Developing and Role Playing Effective Sales Presentations

3rd Edition

A "how-to," step-by-step guide for in-seat and online courses and corporate training programs.

David Sellars, Ph.D.
Davenport University

THOMSON

SOUTH-WESTERN

Australia · Canada · Mexico · Singapore · Spain · United Kingdom · United States

THOMSON

SOUTH-WESTERN

Developing and Role Playing Effective Sales Presentations

Third Edition

David Sellars, PhD

VP/Editorial Director:
Jack W. Calhoun

VP/Editor-in-Chief:
Dave Shaut

Sr. Publisher:
Melissa Acuña

Marketing Manager:
Nicole Moore

Production Editor:
Cliff Kallemeyn

Manufacturing Coordinator:
Sandee Milewski

Design Project Manager:
Michelle Kunkler

Production House:
OffCenter Concept House

Cover Designer:
Rose Alcorn

Cover Image:
© Getty, Inc.

Printer:
Webcom
Toronto, ON

For permission to use material from this
text or product, submit a request online
at http://www.thomsonrights.com.

For more information
contact South-Western,
5191 Natorp Boulevard,
Mason, Ohio 45040.
Or you can visit our Internet site at:
http://www.swlearning.com

My Thanks

I wish to dedicate this book to my colleagues at Davenport University, past and present, for their support and friendship, especially Linda Balkema, Linda Benedict, Tom Brown, Jack Cichy, Randy Flechsig, Bob Funaro, Roy Hamlin, Claudia Hohendorf, Marti Lamphear-Van Horn, Don Maine, Barbara Mieras, Frank Novakowski, Dale Simon, Kathy Sneden, Roger VanderLaan, Al Wetherell, and Colleen Wolfe.

Dave Sellars
Grand Rapids, Michigan

Contents

9   Closing the Sale and Building Customer Relations   105

10   Role Playing and Writing the Complete Sales Presentation   119

Preface

Goals of the First Edition

The first edition of this text was the result of a very unfortunate personal experience. Although I studied marketing for several years in college and even took a course in selling, my first few months as a sales representative for the Pillsbury Company were disastrous. College had not adequately prepared me for a career in sales. It was only by trial and error that I became successful.

When I accepted a teaching position at Davenport University, I searched for a text that would teach my students the sales presentation skills I considered so necessary. None existed, so I developed my own text, which would achieve the following goals:

1. Adapt proven sales presentation and training techniques used in industry to a college selling course.

2. Provide a means for students to build their own sales presentations, using a simple, step-by-step, programmed-learning process, which would ensure that the concepts were applied in the recommended manner.

3. Provide an opportunity for students to learn by doing and to practice sales techniques using extensive role playing exercises.

4. Involve students in evaluating sales presentations to help reinforce the concepts in the text.

5. Design a text that could be effectively used in different ways:

    Primary text in an accelerated course in selling

    Supplemental text in a semester course in selling

    Supplemental text in a sales management course that involves developing sales presentations

    Primary text in a corporate sales training course

I am very happy to report that *Developing and Role Playing Effective Sales Presentations* has been a big success. Over 250 colleges and universities and numerous corporate sales training centers have adopted it. Thousands of students throughout the world have developed sales presentations using the principles in the text. Approximately 2,000 students and sales representatives have completed evaluations of the text and have given it very high ratings. Ninety-five percent said it helped them develop an effective presentation, and 90 percent agreed it was worth the money they paid for it. Virtually all of the instructors who adopted the text were also very enthusiastic about how it enhanced the skill-development process.

Improvements for the Third Edition

The main features that have helped make the previous editions so successful have not been changed. However, my experience as a marketing manager has taught me that one must constantly improve a product for it to stay ahead of competition and meet the needs of a changing marketplace. Numerous improvements have been made in response to suggestions from adopters, reviewers, and students. The following is a list of some of these improvements.

1. The continuing case study has been retained, which features the development of a sales presentation for a product students can relate to—running shoes. Students will follow Jeff Dykehouse, a recently hired sales representative, as he explores the selling process for Fusion running shoes. He is planning a sales call to a manager at a retail sporting goods store. Students will experience the challenge of building a sales presentation and the excitement of closing a sale—from gathering information for the presentation to prospecting and qualifying, and from calling the store manager for an appointment to conducting the presentation and closing the sale.

2. Examples in the text have been updated. More examples for selling services are included so that product and service selling now are given equal treatment.

3. Sections on questioning the prospect and active listening have been expanded.

4. A section has been added to clarify the differences among features, advantages, and benefits. Numerous examples are provided to illustrate how a product or service's features and benefits must be matched up with the prospect's problems and needs.

5. Developing good customer relations through follow-up and service is explained in an expanded section.

6. The process of developing and role playing a sales presentation has been simplified, while the effectiveness of the presentation has been elevated.

7. An Internet assignment has been added for each chapter. Students visit specific Web sites that are designed for professional salespeople. They review features of the site and articles related to selling.

8. Revisions were made to facilitate learning in an online course.

9. The price of the text has been substantially reduced to make it more affordable to students.

Organization

The text begins with an overview of the process of developing a sales presentation and an explanation of the use of role playing to learn how to sell. A section called "Overcoming Fear" is included in Chapter 1 to help students deal with the apprehensions of role playing in class. Examples of products and services that students might select for their projects are provided in Chapter 2. Chapter 3, called "Information Needed for the Sales Presentation," not only details the essential information for the presentation but explains where to obtain it. Prospecting, securing an appointment, and determining the sales call objective are all discussed in Chapter 4. Chapter 5 provides an opportunity for students to identify the features, benefits and visual aids that will be in the presentation.

The main focus of the text is in Chapters 6 through 9, which detail the four parts of an effective sales presentation: Approach, Securing Desire, Handling Objections, and Closing the Sale. Each of these chapters contains an explanation of the steps in the sales presentation and a complete salesperson-prospect dialogue to show how these steps would be used to sell Fusion running shoes. Planning Guides are included in each section so students can apply the steps to their product or service in the recommended manner.

At the end of these four chapters, students are given detailed instructions on how to role play the steps. The instructor can have students role play the Approach, Securing Desire, Handling Objections, and Closing the Sale sections in addition to the complete presentation. If the instructor feels there is not enough time to role play each part, students can role play them on their own, since no lecture is required. In this way, students will be better prepared to role play the complete presentation at the end of the semester. Rating forms are provided for each of the four parts and for the complete presentation to facilitate assessments of role plays. The final chapter, "Role Playing and Writing the Sales Presentation," explains how the role play of the complete presentation will be handled. Content and format of a written report of the sales presentation are also discussed.

Teaching Aids

A comprehensive Instructor's Manual, which includes a test bank and transparency masters, is available to instructors who adopt the text. It contains detailed instructions on how to use role playing to teach the principles of selling. Lesson plans are provided for extensive, moderate, limited, and minimal use of role playing in class, so instructors can choose the amount of role playing that is appropriate for their course objectives.

A videotape is also available to adopters. *Real Selling* contains five programs produced by *Inc.* Magazine. Each program is approximately 25-minutes in length and features actual sales representatives involved in conducting sales calls. The titles are "Preparing for Successful Sales Relationships," "Making Effective Sales Calls," "Dealing with Buying Objections," "The Closing Process," and "Follow-up."

Acknowledgments

I would like to thank all the sales representatives, sales managers, sales trainers, and students I have worked with over the years who have added to my knowledge of selling. I would also like to thank the instructors who reviewed manuscripts and were willing to share their ideas on how to improve this text. Several members of Thomson Learning staff deserve recognition, as well.

David Sellars, Ph.D.

ABOUT THE AUTHOR

David Sellars is a former salesperson, sales trainer, sales manager, marketing manager, and advertising executive, who turned university professor. He has worked for General Motors, Pillsbury, Alberto Culver, Borden Foods, and Bozell & Jacobs Advertising.

He is currently professor of marketing at Davenport University in Grand Rapids, Michigan and teaches professional selling and many other undergraduate and graduate marketing courses. *Developing and Role Playing Effective Sales Presentations* is the product of 30 years spent studying and perfecting selling and role playing techniques. Over 35,000 students and corporate sales representatives have learned how to sell using his innovative training methods. He earned the Davenport University "Outstanding Faculty Award" for his superior teaching abilities and innovative curriculum ideas.

David earned his B.S., M.B.A. and Ph.D. degrees in marketing.

Chapter 1

The Sales Presentation Project

Training Method

Selling is a skill, and, like any skill, you have to actively do it to learn it. Can you imagine trying to learn how to use computer software by just reading about it? It is impossible. This is true of selling too. To learn how to sell, you must experience it. The best training method, short of structured, on-the-job experience, is role playing. You will learn how to sell by using this technique, which is used extensively in industry to train sales representatives.

You will develop a complete sales presentation on a product or service you select and role play it with your instructor or another student acting as a prospect. You will assume the position of an outside sales representative for a manufacturer, wholesaler, service operator, or another company. You are not to assume the position of a salesperson working in a retail store. Outside selling was chosen because it provides more of a challenge and offers a potential for high income and advancement.

The type of presentation approach you will use is called **need-satisfaction selling.** It involves asking questions during the presentation to find out the problems and needs of the prospect, then providing benefits and features of your product or service that will solve the problems or satisfy the needs. Need-satisfaction selling is the approach most business firms use.

How You Will Benefit

The benefits to using *Developing and Role Playing Effective Sales Presentations* are extensive. First, role-playing will allow you to apply the concepts discussed to a real-world situation. You will learn and retain more than you would without role playing—and this course

Looking Ahead

Upon completion of this text and assignments, you should be able to

1. report the steps in an effective sales presentation,

2. develop and role play a professional sales presentation,

3. be more persuasive in communication with others,

4. feel more self-confident in public speaking, and

5. access and learn from articles on the World Wide Web that are written for salespeople.

will be fun. Second, the step-by-step approach and extensive use of examples will better prepare you for role playing. Research conducted by the National Center for Experiential Sales Training has shown that students who used *Developing and Role Playing Effective Sales Presentations* were able to deliver more effective presentations than students who did not. Third, it will take less time to develop a sales presentation because of the detailed, "how to," step-by-step instructions provided. Finally, you will be better prepared to pursue a high-paying career in sales if you so choose.

Overcoming Fear

Most students, when they learn they are going to be involved in role playing, become apprehensive. Their fears result from the fact that they know nothing about developing a sales presentation and have never experienced role playing.

Fear is a natural reaction to new encounters. A certain amount of nervousness under these conditions is good, just as it is in selling. If your adrenaline is going, you are able to think and react more quickly. The key to managing fear is to let it work for you, not against you.

You can overcome excessive fear and build self-confidence three ways. First, you must understand how fear is created. Most people think encountering people or the environment causes fear. This is not true. It is the way *you choose* to react to people and your environment that causes fear. The first time you delivered an oral report in class you probably experienced a lot of fear, yet another student took it in stride. Both of you were speaking to the same people in the same room. The students were receptive and wanted you to do a good job. So it was not the students who caused the fear, it was you. If it were the students, even your instructor would be nervous during a lecture. When you experience fear and anxiety while role playing or preparing to role play, be aware of your fear and ask yourself over and over again, "Do I want to make myself feel this way?" Remember, your instructor and fellow students support you and want you to do a good job.

The second way to overcome fear is to be thoroughly prepared to role play. That's where this text will help. It provides detailed instructions on how to prepare your presentation and role play it. There will be no question in your mind about what you should say and do during a role playing exercise. If you follow the instructions and properly prepare, you will build your self-confidence and you will not be overwhelmed by fear.

Finally, fear can be overcome through experience. *Developing and Role Playing Effective Sales Presentations* will provide you with numerous opportunities to role play your presentation either alone or with others. Try not to be too concerned with fear. When you feel yourself getting uptight about role playing, reread this section. It should help. Also consider talking to your instructor about your fear.

Steps in the Selling Process

The **steps in the selling process** you will be studying are provided next. While *Developing and Role Playing Effective Sales Presentations* focuses on the steps *during* the sales presentation, the other steps are provided here so you understand that the presentation is only a portion of a sales representative's job.

A unique feature of this text is the use of a continuing case study. All of the following steps will be applied to an actual company and product. You will see how Jeff Dykehouse tackles the steps in the selling process for Brooks Shoe, Inc. He sells the Fusion running shoe to Penny Taylor, the manager at a sporting goods store.

Prior to the Sales Presentation

Step 1. Acquire information on your industry, company, product or service, and competition.

Step 2. Develop a list of prospects and acquire information about them.

Step 3. Qualify your prospects.

Step 4. Contact prospects and make appointments.

Step 5. Develop a prospect profile and determine your sales call objective for each prospect.

Step 6. Develop your presentation.

Step 7. Develop an efficient route through your territory.

Step 8. Introduce yourself to the receptionist or secretary and ask to see the decision maker.

During the Sales Presentation

Step 9. Open your presentation with the decision maker.

Step 10. Secure desire for your product or service.

Step 11. Handle objections.

Step 12. Close the sale.

After the Sales Presentation

Step 13. Update prospect and customer records.

Step 14. Build customer relations through follow-up and service.

On the inside front cover of this textbook is a guide called "Steps in a Sales Presentation." It summarizes the steps in each of the four sections of a presentation. You should refer to it when you are preparing to role play.

Concepts To Know

Need-satisfaction selling

Steps in the selling process

Assignments

1. American Marketing Associations (AMA) is an organization serving people in sales and marketing professions. The Web site is http://www.marketingpower.com. Visit the site and review the services offered by AMA. Find an article related to this course by selecting "best practices" then "sales." Develop a report on the site and what you learned from the article. If you do not find a relevant article, go to a college or public library and search databases with full-text articles on selling, such as ABI/Inform. The librarian may have to give you a password to access the database.

2. Study the section, Steps in the Selling Process, in this chapter. Also, skim the chapters in the text. List and discuss ten ways these steps can be applied to conducting an effective search for a new job.

Chapter 2

Choosing a Product or Service

Selection Criteria

Choosing a product or service for your sales presentation is the first step toward the completion of this project. Your selection must meet five criteria:

1. The product or service should be something in which you have a personal interest.

2. An opportunity exists to explore an industry or company that provides future career opportunities.

3. Information needed to construct the presentation is available locally from a representative of the firm. Ideally this person is a salesperson, sales manager, or someone you know well at the firm. (Chapter 3 contains a list of the information needed.)

4. The product or service is currently being marketed and available to customers.

5. The sales call that will be simulated involves outside selling, where the representative travels to the customer location to conduct the presentation.

The sales presentation could involve a product or service related to a hobby. If you enjoy skiing, you could sell a brand of skis to a sporting goods store. If you are a stereo enthusiast, you could sell the model you own to a stereo shop. Perhaps you like clothes. Selling a line of jeans to a clothing retailer would be an excellent choice.

You might wish to choose a product or service that is related to your future career. If you are an advertising major, you could sell radio or television time to a retailer. If you are planning a career in retailing, you could sell a cash register to a buyer for a chain of retail stores. If transportation and distribution are career areas you

Looking Ahead

After studying this chapter and completing the assignments, you should be able to:

1. identify a product or service that is suitable for the sales presentation.

are considering, selling a truck leasing program to a manufacturer would help prepare you for a career in this area. Whatever you choose, it should be something that excites you. Enthusiasm is an important element of a successful presentation. If you are not excited about what you are selling, you cannot expect your prospect to be excited about it and want to buy it.

To be prepared for your presentation, you must have a thorough knowledge of the industry, the product or service you are selling, the company you are selling for, the company and person you are selling to, and the major competitors in your field. This necessitates having access to information in these areas. *The information should be available locally.* If you choose a product or service that is marketed nationally and a representative of the firm is not located in your area, you may not be able to get the information you need in time to meet the deadlines for this project. If the firm is not located in your area, information about its products may be available from a Web site or a distributor or retailer near you.

You may have a parent, relative, friend, or neighbor who is actively involved in outside sales. Selecting their product would ensure access to the information you need. Perhaps you work for a company that has a product or service you could sell. This would also be a good choice. Make sure your selection is currently being marketed. Sufficient information will not be available for a hypothetical product or service. You can always check the Yellow Pages for ideas. Your local chamber of commerce could be helpful too.

If you are selling for a manufacturer or distributor with a line of products, it is generally best to choose one model in the line to sell. Since you will have limited time to role play your complete presentation, you will not have time to present several different products in the line.

Be sure your instructor approves your selection. Make sure it is suitable for a sales call where you meet with the prospect at his or her home or place of business. A presentation that assumes the customer is coming to you, such as in a retail store, is not appropriate. Ask your instructor when he or she expects you to have made a selection. The sooner you decide, the sooner you can begin securing the information you need to develop your presentation.

Product and Service Examples

Here are some examples of products and services that students have used for their presentations.

Product Examples

Sell for . . .	Product	Sell to . . .
Food broker or manufacturer	New food product	Grocery store chain buyer
Office supply distributor	Photocopy or facsimile (FAX) machine	Office manager of a large company
Shoe manufacturer	New brand of shoe	Owner of a shoe store
Tennis racquet distributor or manufacturer	Tennis racquet	Buyer at a sporting goods store
Water ski distributor or manufacturer	Water skis	Buyer at a sporting goods store
Direct sales firm	Household cleaning product	Homeowner
Foodservice wholesaler	New food product	Food and beverage manager of a restaurant
Electronics distributor or manufacturer	Television, stereo, or DVD player	Buyer at an appliance store
Golf equipment distributor or manufacturer	Golf clubs	Manager at a golf shop
Distributor of industrial cleaning products	Cleaning solvent	Purchasing agent at a large manufacturer
Communications equipment distributor	Telephone system	Office manager
Security equipment distributor	Burglar alarm or video surveillance system	Plant security manager at a large manufacturing firm
Greeting cards manufacturer	Greeting cards	Owner of a gift shop
Hardware distributor	Electric drill	Buyer for a chain of hardware stores
College textbook publisher	This textbook on selling	Professor who teaches a professional selling course
Auto parts distributor	Carburetor	Parts manager at a car dealership
Distributor or manufacturer of office partitions	Office partitions	Manager of an office
Hot tub distributor	Hot tub	Homeowner
Sailboard distributor or manufacturer	Sailboard	Owner of a windsport shop
Archery equipment distributor	Hunting bow	Owner of a sporting goods store
Bicycle distributor or manufacturer	Racing bike	Buyer for a chain of bicycle shops
Pharmaceutical manufacturer	Prescription drug	Doctor
Communications equipment distributor	Cellular phone	Real estate agent
Recreational products manufacturer	Tent trailers	Recreational vehicle dealer
Life insurance company	Group life insurance or pension plan for employees	Human resource manager at a large manufacturing firm
Health maintenance organization	Group health plan	Human resource manager
Securities and investments firm	Retirement programs	A business executive

Service Examples

Sell for ...	Service	Sell to ...
Large hotel	Convention facilities and meeting rooms	Sales manager who is planning a sales meeting
Radio or television station	Advertising time	Owner of a retail store
Truck rental or leasing firm	Truck leasing	Distribution manager
Personnel placement agency	Executive recruiting	President of a large firm
Secretarial service	Temporary secretarial help	Human resource manager of an accounting firm
Your college or university	College education	Guidance counselor at a local high school
Construction contractor	Construction of an office building	President of an expanding firm
Travel agency	Executive travel and hotel accommodations	Sales manager
Landscape contractor	Commercial landscaping	President of a firm building a new office complex
Real estate firm	Time-sharing condominiums	A person in their mid-50s
Your local newspaper or college newspaper	Advertising space	Owner of a jeans shop
Outdoor billboard advertising firm	Advertising space	Owner of a car dealership
Freight forwarder	Transporting products to customers	Distribution manager at a steel-fabricating plant
Health club	Physical fitness programs conducted for employees	Human resource manager at a large publishing firm
Florist	Plants to decorate an office	Office manager of a new bank branch
Janitorial service	Cleaning office buildings	Office manager at a law firm
Roofing and siding contractor	Aluminum siding	Homeowner
Accounting and bookkeeping service	Bookkeeping	President of a wholesaling firm
Commercial printing firm	Printing a brochure	Advertising agency
Solar heating contractor	Solar panels	Homeowner
Tour guide	Group tours to Europe	President of a large club
Real estate firm	Listing a house	Homeowner

Assignments

1. The Web site for *Sales and Marketing Management* magazine is http://www.salesandmarketing.com. Visit the site and review the services offered. Articles on selling can be found in two sections noted on the home page: "Current Issues" and "Breaking News." Review both sections and select an article related to this course that does not require a subscription to the magazine. Develop a report on the site and what you learned from the article. If you do not find a relevant article, go to a college or public library and search databases with full-text articles on selling. ABI/Inform is an example. The librarian may have to give you a password to access the databases.

2. Review the product and service examples in the chapter. Identify three potential products or services from different firms that could be the focus of your sales presentation. They must meet all five of the criteria mentioned on page 5. What is the title of the person and type of firm you would be selling to in each case? Secure approval of one of them from your instructor before gathering information for the sales presentation that is discussed in the next chapter.

Chapter 3

Information Needed for the Sales Presentation

What Information Is Needed?

To prepare a sales presentation, you must gather detailed information about the industry your firm participates in, the company you are selling for, the company and person you are selling to, the product or service you are selling, and the competitive product or service you are selling against.

A list of the information you must secure begins on page 12. If the people you meet with consider any of the information confidential, note this in your report. The more information you get, the less time it will take to develop a presentation and the higher the quality of your presentation will be. Do not take any shortcuts or you will pay the price later. The section called "Sources of Information," beginning on page 15, explains where to get the information you need.

Industry Information (the industry your company participates in)

1. What is the size of the total industry in terms of sales? Is the industry growing?

2. What advancements have been made in the industry in recent years?

Refer to pages 15 through 18 for sources of this information.

Looking Ahead

After studying this chapter and completing the assignments, you should be able to:

1. determine the information needed to develop an effective sales presentation,

2. access and review sources that will provide the information needed, and

3. evaluate and record information that can be used in the presentation.

Company Information (the company you are selling for)

1. What is the Web site of the company you are representing? (Review it for information needed for this and the Product/Service section.) What is the history of your company? When was the business founded and who founded it? How has it changed throughout its history? What major accomplishments has the company experienced in recent years?

2. What is the size of the firm in terms of the number of employees and sales (if not confidential)? If this is a publicly held company, secure a copy of its annual report to stockholders. If this is a small company, secure some biographical information about the president and top executives. What qualifications do these individuals possess to manage a successful business?

3. What products or services does the firm offer in its line? Be specific. Secure a catalog, brochure, or list of these products or services. Choose a product or service you will sell for your project.

4. What types of customers buy from this firm? Secure a list of local customers of this firm.

5. Does the firm have branch offices or distribution centers? If so, where are they located?

6. How many sales representatives does the firm employ in the local area? Secure literature that is used to train salespeople. What is considered appropriate attire for salespeople?

7. During what months of the year does the firm enjoy its highest sales?

8. What is the firm's policy on extending credit to its customers? Are payment plans available?

9. If the sales representatives of your company have an order form or contract that customers sign, get a copy of it.

10. Secure photographs of the office building and company personnel.

11. List several reasons why customers should buy from this firm. Be specific.

Refer to pages 15 through 18 for the sources of this information.

Prospect Information (the company and person you are selling to)

1. If you are selling to a business firm, choose an actual local customer your company does business with and gather the following information for that firm.

    A. The firm:

    (1) What is the Web site for this firm? (Review it for information needed for this section.) What type of organization is it (e.g., manufacturer, wholesaler, retailer, service firm)?

    (2) How large is the firm in terms of the number of employees and sales volume (if not confidential)? How long has it been in business?

    (3) What product lines or services does it sell? Be specific.

    (4) Secure any printed material about the company and its products or services, such as booklets, catalogs, and brochures.

    B. The decision maker at this firm:

    (1) Who makes the buying decisions for your product or service at this firm? What are the person's major responsibilities and job title?

    (2) Refer to the discussion of problems and needs in Chapter 5, beginning on page 27. What are the problems and needs of this firm, and how can your product or service solve the problems or satisfy the needs? Be as detailed and specific as possible. Identify several problems and needs. What is the most important problem or need?

(3) How will your product or service be used by the prospect?

C. If you are selling a product to a retailer, who will resell it to the ultimate consumer (e.g., food product or stereo), gather the following information:

(1) What are the characteristics of the typical consumer, such as age, income, education, gender, family status, and occupation?

(2) What problems or needs does the consumer have that are related to your product? Be as detailed as possible. Identify several problems and needs. What is the most important problem or need?

2. If you are selling directly to the ultimate consumer, answer the questions in section C above. The "ultimate consumer" is someone who buys a product or service for his or her own personal consumption. For example, a salesperson selling roofing to a homeowner or a financial advisor who is selling a retirement program to person nearing retirement is selling to the ultimate consumer.

Refer to pages 15 through 18 for sources of information.

Product/Service Information (what you are selling)

1. General information:

A. Have sales for the product or service that is the focus of your presentation been growing or declining? By how much?

B. Does the firm offer any warranties or guarantees? Get samples of the warranty or guarantee statements.

C. What price does your firm charge for its product or service? What discounts are offered? Secure a price list.

D. How quickly can your company deliver its products or perform its service from the date the order is taken?

E. What are the typical reasons your company's customers give for not buying the product or service? Identify several. How does the salesperson resolve each customer objection?

F. What sources do salespeople use to prove that the product offers desirable benefits to customers (e.g., marketing research studies, product or user tests, test-market data, and endorsements from authorities or prominent people in the industry)? Secure some letters sent to your company from satisfied customers (i.e., testimonial letters). Ask a salesperson with your company to tell you about two local customers who have had good results with the product or service (case histories). Find out the specific details, including who, what, when, where, and how.

G. What visual and audio aids do your salespeople use during sales presentations, which are not mentioned elsewhere in this chapter (e.g., charts, graphs, flip charts, slides, and posters)? Get samples of them.

H. What advertising does the firm do, including co-op advertising? Get samples of the advertisements. Refer to the discussion of features and benefits in Chapter 5 beginning on page 28. List the features and benefits mentioned in the ads.

I. What is the size of the average customer purchase in dollars and units?

J. What services does your company offer its customers after a sale is made, including the services its sales representatives provide? What are the specific features and benefits of these services? Be as detailed as possible.

K. What are the typical problems customers have had after the sale is made? How does your company correct these problems?

2. If you are selling an intangible service:

   A. What activities does the service include? Explain each in detail. How does your firm customize the service to meet the specific needs of its customers?

   B. What qualifications do the employees of this firm have that enables them to provide high-quality service? This would include past training and years of experience providing the service.

   C. Where is your service located?

   D. What are the features and benefits of the above activities, employee qualifications, and location? Be specific.

3. If you are selling a tangible product:

   A. What is the history of the product? When was it first introduced? What major improvements have been made in recent years?

   B. What are the physical characteristics of the product, including how it is made, the materials/ingredients it contains, and how it performs? What quality control procedures are used during manufacturing? What are the features and benefits of these factors?

   C. Can your product be demonstrated to prospective customers? If so, how?

   D. Get a sample, scale model, cross section, or photograph of the product. Secure a specification sheet that describes details of the product.

   E. If you are selling the product to a retailer, who will resell it to the ultimate consumer:

      (1) What is the suggested retail price? What is the percentage of markup and profit margin per unit?

      (2) What turnover rate can the retailer expect on your product?

      (3) What sales promotion programs does your firm offer, including point-of-sale material, contests, sweepstakes, coupons, sampling, and premiums? Get specific details and examples of each.

      (4) What product and sales training programs does your company make available to its retailers or dealers?

Refer to the sources of information on pages 15 through 18.

Competitor Information (what the prospect might buy or is currently buying that competes with your product or service)

1. General information:

   A. Who are your firm's main competitors? Identify one where information about the firm is readily available. Secure the information that follows for this competitor. Some of the information may be available on the firm's Web site.

   B. When was the competitor's firm founded? Has your company been in business longer? What is the size of the competitor in relationship to your firm? Is it growing more quickly or more slowly than your firm? Why? If this is a publicly held company, secure a copy of its annual report.

   C. What is the competitor's policy on extending credit to its customers? Are your firm's policies more or less liberal?

   D. What price does your competitor charge for its product or service? Secure a price list. What discounts are offered? How do these factors compare to your product or service?

   E. How quickly can your competitor deliver its product or perform its service in comparison with your firm?

   F. What services does the competitor offer its customers after a sale is made? How are your services superior or inferior?

G. Secure copies of catalogs, brochures, charts, graphs, and any other printed materials that are available.

H. What are your competitor's major strengths and weaknesses?

2. If you are selling an intangible service:

A. What activities does the competitor service include? List several. Explain each in detail. How do they compare with those your firm offers?

B. What qualifications and experience do the competitor employees have? How are your employees more or less qualified to serve customers?

C. Where is the service firm located? Is your firm in a more convenient location for customers?

3. If you are selling a tangible product:

A. What is the history of the competitor's product? When was it first introduced? What major improvements have been made in recent years?

B. What products does the competitor offer that your firm also offers or does not offer?

C. Secure a sample and specification sheet containing details of the competitor's product. How is your product superior and inferior in terms of features and benefits? What is the price of the competitor's product? How does it compare to your price?

D. If you are selling a product to a retailer, who will resell it to the ultimate consumer:

(1) What is the percentage of markup and profit margin per unit your competitor offers retailers? How does it compare with yours?

(2) How does the turnover rate of your product compare with that of your competitor's product?

(3) What advertising support for the product does the competitor employ? How does it compare with yours? Get examples of the advertisements. List the features and benefits mentioned in the ads.

(4) What sales promotion programs does your competitor offer its customers? How do they compare with yours?

(5) What training programs does your competitor offer its retailers? How do they compare with yours?

Refer to the information that follows for the sources of this information.

Sources of Information

The information needed to develop an effective presentation, listed on the previous pages, can be obtained from personal interviews, company literature and Web sites, and electronic and library sources.

Interview Sources—Company Personnel

The primary source of information for your presentation will be personal interviews with representatives of the company for which you are selling. Meet with several people who work for your company, including sales representatives, sales managers, marketing personnel, and even the company president. Explain the nature of this project and ask them the questions listed on the previous pages. Consider spending a day with a representative and observe him or her during actual sales calls. Also, ask to go on a tour of the company's facilities.

Approximately one-third of the needed information concerns the prospect you will be contacting and your competitor. Ask your company personnel to identify a local customer who can be your prospect and one major competitor. Your company may be able to supply adequate information concerning these companies, their competitors. In all probability, however, you will have to interview sales and marketing people who work for these firms. As a last resort, call these companies and request the information needed.

Since you do not want to inconvenience the people you meet with any more than necessary, you will want to gather as much information as you can in the shortest amount of time possible. It is *strongly recommended* that you audio tape the conversations you have so you do not have to waste time taking notes. Take a tape recorder with you and enough tape for at least two hours of recording. *Ask for permission to tape the interviews.*

When you meet with your sources, it is important that you present a professional image and dress appropriately for these meetings. Men should wear a sports coat and tie. Women should wear a dress, skirt, or suit. Treat it like a job interview. Many students have gotten job offers from the very companies they have used for their projects. Be on time for all appointments, and meet with your sources well in advance of the due date for this part of the project, because business people often have to reschedule appointments due to unforeseen commitments. You will have to find your own transportation for these meetings and be prepared to meet with your sources more than once.

Company Literature and Web Site Sources

A wealth of information for your report can be secured from printed literature available from your company, prospect, and competitor. Review the visual aids and proof sources requested in the "Company Information," "Product/Service Information," and "Competitor Information" sections. Answers to many of the questions can be found in this literature. Also review Web sites that your company, prospect, and competitor may have.

Electronic Sources

In addition to your company, prospect, and competitor Web sites, the electronic sources below may have valuable information. Also, ask a librarian what databases contain information listed in this chapter.

Numerous links to sites with valuable information:

> *CI Strategies and Tools.*
> http://www.fuld.com/i3/index.html

Economic and industry data for the United States, the state, and local areas:

> *U.S. Small Business Administration.*
> http://www.sbaonline.sba.gov

Demographic information of consumers for the U.S., the state, and local areas:

> *U.S. Census Bureau.* http://www.census.gov

How to access financial reports of companies:

> *Annual Reports Online.*
> http://www.zpub.com/sf/arl

Search engines such as:
> http://www.google.com and
> http://www.yahoo.com

Library Sources

Most of the industry information and some of the company, prospect, product/service, and competitor information can be found in a college, university, or local library. Review the following print sources.

> *Industry Surveys.* Standard & Poor's. New York: Standard & Poor's. Industry trends and information on companies.

> *Encyclopedia of Associations.* The Gale Group. Farmington Hills, MI: The Gale Group. Trade associations for your industry. Call appropriate associations and request information.

> *Hoover's Handbook of American Business.* Austin, TX: Hoover's Business Press. Histories and sales for hundreds of companies.

> *International Directory of Company Histories.* Detroit: St. James Press. Histories and sales for hundreds of companies.

> *Standard & Poor's Register of Corporations, Directors & Executives.* Charlottesville, VA:

Robinson Hall
Davenport University
415 East Fulton
Grand Rapids, MI 49503
May 14, 20__

Mr. John Gertz
Senior Sales Representative
Wyman Distributing Company
3510 Division Avenue
Grand Rapids, MI 49506

Dear Mr. Gertz:

Please accept my sincere appreciation for all the assistance you gave me with my project for my "Principles of Selling" class. I realize you are a very busy man and you had to spend a lot of time providing me with the information I needed.

The meetings we had were both interesting and very informative. I especially want to thank you for allowing me to accompany you on several sales calls. It was exciting for me to see how the concepts I'm learning in class are applied in the real world. The product sample and visual aids you loaned me were very helpful, too.

As a result of my class project and my meetings with you, I am seriously considering a career in sales. It looks like it would be fun and provide me with substantial financial rewards if I apply what I have learned in this class.

Thank you again for your time and the knowledge you shared with me.

Sincerely,

Debbie Johnson

Debbie Johnson, Student
Davenport University

Debbie Johnson
Robinson Hall
Davenport University
415 East Fulton
Grand Rapids, MI 49503

Mr. John Gertz
Senior Sales Representative
Wyman Distributing Company
3510 Division Avenue
Grand Rapids, MI 49506

(Use a business-size envelope that measures 4-1/4" × 9-1/2")

Standard & Poor's. Company addresses and other details.

Household Spending: Who Spends How Much on What? Ithaca, NY: New Strategist Publications. Spending habits for different customer groups and hundreds of products and services.

Best Customers: Demographics of Consumer Demand. Ithaca, NY: New Strategist. The most desirable customers for hundreds of products and services.

Yellow Pages telephone directory. All companies in your local area listed by type of business.

"Thank You" Letters

The people you will be meeting with are busy. Typically, they enjoy meeting with college students, but it does take up their time. To show your appreciation for their time, your instructor may want you to send each one a "thank you" letter. The letters must be typed on 8 1/2 × 11 paper and mailed in #10 business-size envelopes. Put a stamp on each one. Be sure to word process the envelopes, too. Make sure there are no typographical, spelling, or grammatical errors, and do not forget to sign the letter in ink. Your instructor may wish to see the letters before they are mailed. If so, put the letters in the envelopes, but do not seal them. An example of a letter and envelope is provided on page 17.

Assignments

1. Pi Sigma Epsilon is an organization that serves sales and marketing professionals. The Web site is http://www.pse.org. Visit the site and review programs offered. Find an article related to this course by selecting "Newsletter." Develop a report on the site and what you learned from the article. If you do not find a relevant article, go to a college or public library and search databases with full-text articles on selling. ABI/Inform is an example. The librarian may have to give you a password to access the databases.

2. Secure all the information that is discussed in the chapter for your sales presentation.

3. Prepare a typed report of the above information including a bibliography.

4. Prepare "thank you" letters and envelopes, following the guidelines and format discussed on pages 17 and 18, for anyone who provided information for the sales presentation. Your instructor must review them before mailing.

Chapter 4

Prospecting and the Preapproach

Prospecting

Before a salesperson can begin making sales calls, he or she must identify potential customers. This process is called **prospecting.** In some industries, potential customers are well defined and easy to identify. The manufacturer of packaged food products would call on grocery and convenience stores. A firm selling a printing service could call on advertising agencies. However, determining whom to call on if you are selling life insurance, meeting rooms and convention facilities, or aluminum siding for homes would be more challenging. Some salespeople spend as much as 80 percent of their time prospecting.

If you were hired to represent Brooks Shoe, Inc., in your state, who would you call on to sell a new running shoe called Fusion? Shoe stores and sporting goods stores might come to mind, but which specific stores? What are the store names, addresses, and telephone numbers? What are the names of the buyers? What sources would you explore to identify these stores? Your first source would be the list of current customers Brooks would give you. A trade publication called *Sporting Goods Buyers' Directory* would also be a good source. It lists all the sporting goods stores in the United States, by state and city. Store names, addresses, telephone numbers, and buyers' names are also provided. You might identify some prospects as you are driving around your territory. National and regional sporting goods trade shows can be an excellent source for prospects. Finally, some of your current customers may open new stores. These are possible prospects, provided they are located in your territory.

Looking Ahead

After studying this chapter and completing the assignments, you should be able to:

1. report how to get new customers for a firm and secure appointments with prospects,

2. develop a profile of a prospect, and

3. determine your sales call objective.

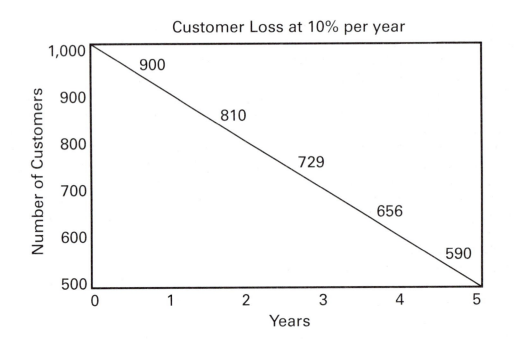

Customer Loss at 10% per year

Prospecting must be a continuous process, because salespeople lose customers even if they represent excellent companies and sell superior products or services. Customers may move out of their territory, buyers may change jobs, competitors may take customers, and customers may become bad credit risks or even go out of business. Most firms lose 10 to 25 percent of their customers each year. If a firm had 1,000 customers today, lost only 10 percent each year, and did not replace any, it would have only 590 customers in five years. This is illustrated in the above figure.

Qualifying

Qualifying is the process of gathering information about a potential customer to determine if it is worthwhile to make a face-to-face sales presentation. Specifically, you are trying to determine whether the customer has a potential need for your product or service, has the financial resources to pay for it, will purchase quantities large enough to make the customer profitable, and has the authority to make a purchase decision. It would be a waste of time to call on a firm that did not meet these four criteria. The information gathered while qualifying a potential cus-

tomer has the added benefit of helping you plan what to say during the sales call. A potential customer, who has been qualified, is called a **prospect**.

The Preapproach

The **preapproach** involves securing an appointment to make the presentation, developing a profile of the prospect, determining your sales call objective, and planning the presentation. Some of the process of planning the presentation is discussed in this chapter. Other issues are covered extensively in Chapters 5 through 9.

Securing the Appointment

Before you can make a sales presentation, you must secure an appointment with the prospect. In some cases, this can be more challenging than convincing a prospect to buy. There are three methods salespeople use to secure appointments. They are cold calling in person, telephone prospecting, and sending a letter of introduction followed by a telephone call.

Cold calling in person involves walking into a prospect's place of business without an appointment. An advantage to cold calling is that you can reduce travel time by calling on all the businesses in an area. Cold calling is also an effective method of getting appointments with prospects who will not grant them over the telephone. Qualifying and profiling information can be gathered on cold calls as well.

There are, however, many disadvantages to this method of getting appointments. Some prospects will not see salespeople without an appointment. In such cases, the most you can hope for on a cold call is to secure an appointment for a later date. Cold calling is very time-consuming. Prospects may not be available when you arrive. Finally, cold calling may not be appropriate if you are selling certain things, such as high-priced, technical products or services, including computer software and health insurance. Prospects in these fields may consider cold calling to be unprofessional.

An increasing number of salespeople who call on businesses secure appointments by first arranging a meeting over the telephone. At this writing, no laws exist that prohibit this use of telemarketing. **Telephone prospecting** is inexpensive and less time-consuming than cold calling because you can cover a large number of geographically dispersed prospects in a relatively short time. Disadvantages to this method are that it is easier for a prospect to say "no" on the telephone than in person, and you do not have the benefit of observing the prospect's nonverbal communications. Furthermore, some salespeople have difficulty dealing with rejection on the telephone. Ten telephone calls might result in talking to four decision makers, with one consenting to an appointment.

A procedure that will increase the productivity of telephone prospecting is sending a **letter of introduction** prior to the call. The letter will prepare the prospect for the call and help convey a professional image for you and your company. Referring to the letter during the telephone call will also help you establish a rapport.

The purpose of the letter should be to get the prospect's attention and to arouse interest in and anticipation of your telephone call. It must be addressed to a specific individual and should focus on one or two important benefits. Do not disclose too much information. The letter is intended to increase your chance of securing an appointment, not to close the sale. A sample letter of introduction that tries to get an appointment for Brooks with a retail sporting goods buyer appears on page 22. The salesperson is selling Fusion, a new running shoe, to a retail store.

A dialogue of a telephone call between Jeff Dykehouse, the salesperson trying to sell Fusion, and Penny Taylor, the manager of the sporting goods store, is provided next to help illustrate what a call might sound like. Assume she was sent the letter on page 22 prior to the call.

JEFF: Ms. Taylor?

PROSPECT: Yes.

JEFF: My name is Jeff Dykehouse from Brooks Shoe Company. How are you today?

PROSPECT: Pretty good.

JEFF: Last Monday, I sent you a letter concerning our exciting new running shoe called Fusion. Do you remember seeing it?

PROSPECT: Yes.

JEFF: You'll recall that in the letter I mentioned Fusion has a new patented feature that will improve the running performance of your customers while reducing injuries. I'm calling to see when we can get together to explain how Fusion will increase your athletic shoes sales and profits.

Ms. Taylor, are mornings or afternoons best for you?

PROSPECT: We don't need any more running shoes right now.

JEFF: You are definitely in a position to know if you need any new products, Ms. Taylor. However, the real question is whether you are open to a product that is a true breakthrough in running shoe technology, one that your customers will love and that will provide more profits for your store.

January 22, 20__

Ms. Penny Taylor
Taylor Sports, Inc.
2122 Main Street
Grand Rapids, MI 49507

Dear Ms. Taylor:

Are your customers looking for an athletic shoe that will improve running performance and reduce foot, ankle, and leg injuries? Are you looking for a shoe that will generate more profits for your store?

Brooks is about to launch a revolutionary new running shoe called Fusion. Perhaps you have read about Fusion in the trade press or heard that it recently won the "Best Running Shoe" award at the EXSL show in Europe. Fusion has a special patented feature, which is a breakthrough in running shoe technology.

The whole story is especially exciting. In the next week, I'll call you to arrange a time to show you Fusion. When we meet, I will also explain the details of our comprehensive marketing program, planned to support Fusion, and show how it will increase your athletic shoe sales and profits.

Sincerely,

Jeffery Dykehouse

Jeffery Dykehouse

Would next Tuesday or Wednesday morning be more convenient for you?

PROSPECT: I guess I could meet with you on Wednesday at 10:30.

JEFF: Great! Your office is located at 2122 Main Street, right?

PROSPECT: Yes. That's right.

JEFF: I look forward to meeting you next Wednesday at 10:30, Ms. Taylor.

You Are Selling . . .	Sales Call Objective
An employee fitness program to the human resource director of a large firm	Convince the prospect to buy 10 health club memberships for the firm's top executives with fitness evaluations to be conducted in the next two weeks.
A sales training workshop to a district sales manager	Convince the prospect to schedule a two-day workshop for 27 new and experienced sales representatives during the week of November 15.
An industrial cleaning solvent to a purchasing agent at a large manufacturer	Convince the prospect to buy a sample quantity of Quick-Cleen for testing, accept delivery by next week, and have the test completed by the end of the month.
A new prescription drug to a doctor	Convince the doctor to accept 50 free samples of Inoxcine today, begin dispensing the samples to patients, and begin prescribing the medication through patients' pharmacies immediately.
A new food product to the food and beverage manager of a restaurant	Convince the prospect to buy 5 cases of Bostonian Frozen Shrimp, accept delivery by Friday, and add the item to the menu immediately.
Meeting room facilities to a sales manager who is planning a sales meeting	Convince the prospect to accompany me to my hotel this week to see the meeting rooms and sample various items on our luncheon menu.
College education to a high school counselor	Convince the prospect to bring 20 high school students to my campus by the end of the month for a tour, orientation, and lunch.
A new food product to a grocery store chain buyer	Convince the prospect to buy 20 cases per store of Pep, display the product on the shelf in the diet section of the store, price it $1.79, and accept delivery by next week.
Construction services to the president of a firm that is planning to build an addition to its plant	Convince the prospect to allow my firm to submit a bid this month for the construction.
Radio ads to the owner of a clothing store	Convince the prospect to sign a contract for 50 thirty-second radio spots to air next month.
A prepackaged tour of Europe to the assistant minister of a large church.	Convince the prospect to allow me to make a slide presentation this month to people in the congregation who are interested in the vacation.
A fleet of automobiles to a sales manager of a large manufacturer	Convince the prospect to accompany me to my dealership this week to test ride the Honda Accord.
Group life insurance to the human resource manager of a large manufacturer	Convince the prospect to allow me to do a needs analysis of the firm this week so I can present a group life plan by the first of the month.

Developing a Profile of the Prospect

The type of presentation you are developing is called **need-satisfaction selling**. The entire presentation revolves around *specific* prospect's needs. It is customized and reflects the prospect's personality, current situation, purchases of competitor products and services, and problems. To customize a presentation, you must know something about the firm and the individual you are calling on before planning the presentation and making the sales call. A **prospect profile** must be completed. This profile will result in asking the right questions and providing the appropriate features and benefits during the presentation, which will increase the probability that you will close the sale.

Gathering profiling information before the sales call is challenging because often it is not readily available. Secondary sources on pages 16 and 18 can be explored. Primary sources include current customers, competitor sales representatives, receptionists and secretaries at the prospect's place of business, and the actual prospect. Some profile information cannot be secured until the sales call. The more information that can be gathered before the initial call, the greater the chances of the call being successful.

Companies often provide their salespeople with a prospect profile form. The one on page 25 is for Brooks. Study it thoroughly so that you can gain a better understanding of the continuing case.

Determining the Sales Call Objective

Before you meet with your prospect, you must decide what you hope to achieve during the sales call. This is called the **sales call objective**. Think of it as a target. To hit a target you must be able to see it. Even a world champion archer cannot hit a target unless he or she can see it. So the sales call objective should be written down before each call. It requires a commitment from the prospect and should be specific and measurable. It also must include a time frame indicating when action will take place. Following is the sales call objective for Fusion. Other examples are provided on page 23 to help you develop your own sales call objective.

Fusion Sales Call Objective: Convince the retailer to buy 18 pairs of the Fusion running shoe, price them at $124.95 per pair, and accept delivery by the first of next month.

In the space provided below, write the sales call objective for your product or service. Be sure it involves a commitment from the prospect.

My Sales Call Objective Is:

Planning the Sales Presentation

A sales call must be well planned if it is going to be successful. The information to communicate during the call must be gathered and organized in a logical sequence in order to change the prospect from being unaware of your company and product or service to being a willing buyer. Appropriate questions must be identified to ascertain the prospect's current situation and needs. Visual aids must be developed to enhance your ability to communicate your message. Questions and resistance the prospect might offer must be anticipated. Everything you plan to say and do must be determined ahead of time. Final preparation involves practicing the presentation before the call.

The next few chapters will help you plan your sales presentation. Chapter 5 provides an opportunity to identify the needs and problems of your prospect, determine features and benefits to offer that appeal to the needs, and construct visual aids that will improve the effectiveness of communications.

The sales presentation is divided into four sections: Approach, Securing Desire, Handling Objections, and Closing the Sale. In Chapter 6, on

Brooks Prospect Profile

Company Name: _____ Taylor Sports, Inc _____

Address: ___2122 Main Street_____

___Grand Rapids, MI_____ Zip Code: ___49507_____

Telephone Number: ___(616) 555-2122_____

Location/Direction/Travel Time: _____Route 67 to Trobridge exit. North on Trobridge_

two miles to Lakewood Shopping Plaza. Travel Time—1 hour 15 minutes_____

_____

Company Sales Volume: _N.A._____ Number of Stores: __1_____

Years in Business: __6 months_____ Credit Rating: _N.A._____

Decision Maker's Name/Title: __Ms. Penny Taylor, owner with Bill Winston_____

_____

Major Responsibilities: _Manages the store and buys athletic shoes._____

_(Bill buys other products.)_____

Personal Qualities of Decision Maker: __Sounded like a dominant personality on the phone.

_____

Best Time to See: _Tuesday and Wednesday mornings_____

Names/Titles of Others Who Influence Buying Decisions: __None_____

_____

Secretary's Name: ___None_____

Current Shoe Lines: __Nike, Asics, Etonic, and Reebok. The store has never_____

_ordered from Brooks._____

Target Market: _This is a specialty sporting goods store that appeals to the_____

_serious recreational athlete._____

Trading Area: __Ten-mile radius of the store_____

Problems/Needs: _Increase sales and profits, generate more store traffic, stock_____

_running shoes that appeal to the serious runner_____

the Approach, you will learn how to introduce yourself to the prospect, establish a rapport, gain his or her interest and attention, and begin to gather information related to his or her current situation. Chapter 7, "Securing Desire," is where the body of the presentation is discussed. Specific prospect problems and needs are identified and supported with features and benefits. Chapter 8 is called "Handling Objections." You will identify the resistance your prospect may offer and learn how to overcome it. Chapter 9, on "Closing the Sale," will provide insight on how to ask for a commitment. Plenty of examples are included to help you step-by-step through the process of building your presentation. Opportunities will also be presented for you to practice the presentation using sophisticated role playing techniques.

Concepts to Know

Prospecting

Qualifying

Prospect

Preapproach

Cold calling

Telephone prospecting

Letter of introduction

Need-satisfaction selling

Prospect profile

Sales call objective

Assignments

1. Sales and Marketing Executives International (SMEI) is a professional organization for salespeople. Their Web site is http://www.smei.org. Review the site and note the services offered. Find an article related to this course that does not require a subscription to their publication. Search for articles under "Marketing Library." Develop a report on the site and what you learned in the article. If you do not find a relevant article, go to a college or public library and search databases with full-text articles on selling. ABI/Inform is an example. The librarian may have to give you a password to access to databases.

2. Construct a typed letter of introduction that could be mailed to your prospect before the sales call.

3. Write the sales call objective for your presentation. Make sure it involves a commitment from the prospect.

Chapter 5

Appealing to Prospect Needs

Prospect and Consumer Problems and Needs

Since the type of presentation you are developing is called *need-satisfaction selling,* the entire presentation revolves around the prospect's needs and problems. The first step in this approach is to identify the **prospect's needs**. These are gaps between his or her current situation and the ideal situation. Specific needs the prospect might have must be identified before the presentation can be developed. The following are some examples of needs a retail sporting goods buyer and consumer might have related to Fusion running shoes. Also, there is an example of needs a salesperson and sales manager might have related to a sales training workshop. A training consulting firm is selling the workshop to a sales manager who is considering a training program for his or her sales representatives.

Fusion Running Shoes

Problems/needs of the final user (serious runner)

1. Improve running performance

2. Have greater comfort

3. Reduce foot, ankle, and knee injuries

4. Enjoy running more

5. Improve health, fitness, and sex appeal

6. Receive good value in relation to price

Looking Ahead

After studying this chapter and completing the assignments, you should be able to:

1. identify the needs of a prospect and the features, advantages, and benefits inherent in your product or service that correspond to the needs,

2. provide proof of benefits to overcome the prospect's skepticism, and

3. develop and effectively use dramatization and visual aids during a presentation.

Problems/needs of the reseller (retail store manager)

1. Increase sales, profits, and turnover

2. Offer high-quality products that satisfy consumer needs

3. Buy from a dependable company, which has knowledgeable, service-oriented salespeople

4. Generate more store traffic

5. Receive advertising support and promotional discounts

Sales Training Workshop

Problems/needs of the final user (workshop participants—salespeople)

1. Increase territory sales and personal income

2. Gain hands-on knowledge of successful selling techniques

3. Improve management of time resulting in more leisure time with family and friends

4. Experience an exciting presentation of workshop material

Problems/needs of the intermediary (sales manager)

1. Increase company sales and profits

2. Improve effectiveness of sales training

3. Reduce time and costs to train sales representatives

4. Provide a comprehensive training program relevant for both new and veteran salespeople

Features, Advantages, and Benefits

Once the prospect problems and needs have been identified, you can present the features, advantages, and benefits related to the problems and needs.

Features—physical characteristics of a company or product or description of a service. Features are facts about your company, product, or service. They may be tangible, such as the materials your product is made of, including size, color, or shape. Examples of intangible features are fast delivery, knowledgeable service personnel, and technical support. Features answer the prospect's question, "What is it?"

Advantages—what the features will do. If a feature of a product is that it is made of stainless steel, the advantage is that it will not rust.

Benefits—favorable results the prospect will enjoy from the features. Benefits are derived from features and explain what the features do for the prospect. They relate features to the prospect and answer the question, "What's in it for me?" People are motivated to buy based on benefits, not features, so you should mention features in your presentation but stress the benefits.

One technique to help you distinguish among feature, advantage, and benefit statements is to try to put them in the following sentence. This has . . . (feature) . . . so that . . . (advantage) . . . , which means you . . . (benefit).

> "This has *stainless steel parts* so that *it will not rust,* which means you *reduce replacement cost and save money.*"

Many trainers use the acronym "**FAB**" to help salespeople remember to present Features, Advantages, and Benefits. "FAB" will be used throughout this text.

Examples of features, advantages, and benefits for the running shoe Fusion are on page 30. Note how the features and benefits correspond with the problems and needs discussed earlier. Also provided are features, advantages, and benefits of a sales training workshop. A salesperson for a consulting firm is intending to present the workshop to a sales manager.

Propelled into the Future...

Fusion: A blending, a coalition. The future has arrived with the Brooks Fusion. The Fusion is the alternative in athletic shoes, combining the cushioning features of HydroFlow® with the performance enhancement technology of the Brooks Propulsion Plate.

The benefit of the Propulsion Plate is that it works throughout the three phases of forward motion: heel strike, midstance, and toe-off. The stability component and external arch support function together to provide smooth transitions from phase one through phase three.

The plate design incorporates a rearfoot stability component, an external arch support, and a forefoot propulsion component that complement the natural spring mechanism of the foot.

The profile of this design is engineered to work synergistically with muscle function and improve biomechanical efficiency for the athlete.

In running, an athlete experiences two load peaks. The first is upon initial foot impact. The second is associated with foot propulsion as the heel is lifted off the ground and the load is shifted to the metatarsal heads of the forefoot.

With the Brooks Propulsion Plate, the velocity and degree of pronation are controlled, while shock is attenuated and potential energy is stored by the external arch support. As the heel is lifted off the ground, the energy is released from the external arch support and assists in bending the forefoot Propulsion Plate as the load is transferred to the metatarsal heads. Throughout the toe-off phase, the energy stored in the forefoot plate is released to provide propulsion into the next stride.

These advancements in the Midsole Concept are further evidence of Brooks' commitment to developing technologically advanced, anatomically correct athletic footwear.

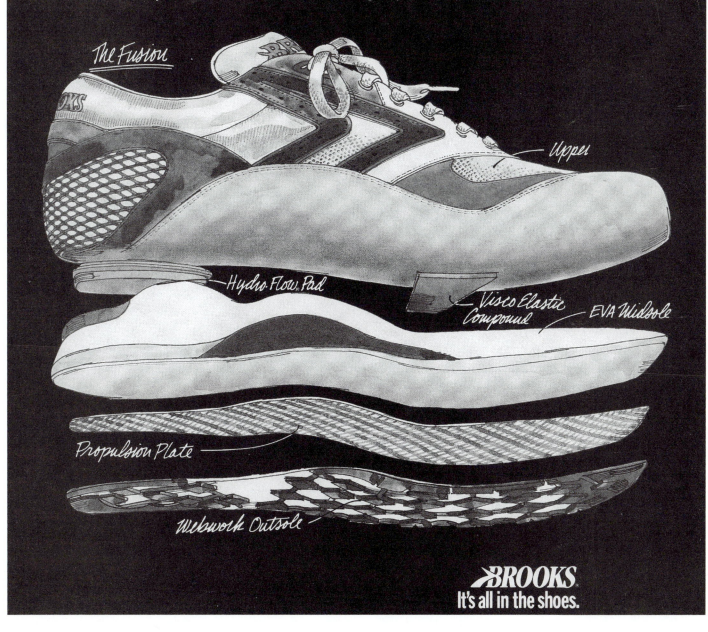

The Fusion

Upper

Hydro Flow Pad

Visco Elastic Compound

EVA Midsole

Propulsion Plate

Webwork Outsole

Fusion Running Shoes

Features	Advantages	Benefits
Final User (Serious runner)		
1. Fusion has a carbon-fiber Propulsion Plate System	Upon impact, the energy stored in the front of the Propulsion Plate System is released to propel the runner into the next stride.	The performance of the runner is improved so he or she can run faster, with less exertion.
2. A dual-chamber HydroFlow pad is in the heel of the shoe.	Shocks from running are absorbed in the shoe rather than by the body.	Foot, ankle, and knee injuries are reduced.
Reseller (Retail buyer)		
1. The suggested retail price for Fusion is $124.95 with a markup of 46 percent.	The profit margin per unit is $57.95.	The retailer will increase athletic shoe profits.
2. The introductory promotional campaign includes national advertising, point-of-sale material, and brochures.	Consumer awareness of the product will be created.	Store traffic, sales, and profits will be maximized.

Sales Training Workshop

Features	Advantages	Benefits
Final User (Salespeople in the workshop)		
1. Participants develop and role play sales presentations on their specific products or services.	Ensures concepts are used properly. Training is hands-on.	Salespeople will conduct more effective presentations resulting in higher territory sales and personal income.
2. Films, case histories, and simulations are used throughout the workshop.	The interest and attention levels will be high.	Participants will learn and retain more.
Intermediary (Sales manager)		
1. Over 3,000 salespeople from 400 companies have completed the workshop.	The concepts and methods tested and have been refined, so the training is state-of-the-art.	You are guaranteed to get results in increased sales and profits.
2. The workshop begins with a skills assessment of each participant.	Salesperson strengths and weaknesses are identified.	The training will be effective, since it focuses on overcoming participant weaknesses. Both new and veteran salespeople will benefit.

We said earlier that the process of persuading a prospect to want to buy your product or service involves first identifying the prospect's needs and then matching those needs to appropriate features and benefits. You may have 10 to 20 features and benefits, but only a few may match a particular prospect's needs. The following figure illustrates a situation in which the prospect has four specific needs, but the salesperson has 16 features and benefits he or she could present. Rather than overwhelming the prospect with a discussion of all 16 benefits, the salesperson should present only those related to the needs. Remember, your mission during a presentation is to appeal to this prospect's *specific* buying motives, not to impress him or her with how much you know about your company and product.

Four Prospect
Needs

Sixteen Features
and Benefits

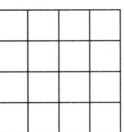

Features and
Benefits/Needs Match

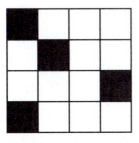

Proving Benefits

A prospect is typically skeptical of a salesperson's claims about the benefits of the product or service, especially if the prospect does not know the salesperson. Therefore, you must provide **proof** of the benefits in order to build trust and to convince the prospect that what you say is true. The following are some types of proof.

Company-supplied proof, such as Research and Development department reports, product or user tests, marketing research studies, company specification sheets, guarantees, warrantees, sales data on your company and product or service, and a list of current customers.

Independent research findings from marketing research firms, articles published in trade journals and newspapers, government data, *Consumer Reports* ratings, and Underwriters' Laboratories test results.

Testimonial letters from satisfied customers. When you present these letters, first establish the credibility of the authors. Quote some of the important sections of the letters. Finally, relate the customer's situation to that of this prospect.

Endorsements from experts or prominent people, such as a nationally known physician who recommends a diet food or a sports celebrity who wears Nike basketball shoes.

Case history, which is a story about another company that had good results from using your product or service. Discuss who, what, when, where, how, and any other specific details of the successful results.

Demonstration, for example, encouraging a prospect to smell and taste a food product, to sit in an office chair being sold, to type on a word processor, or to accept a free trial offer of a product or service.

This listing is in increasing order of believability. Company-supplied proof is the least convincing, a demonstration, the most convincing. If you are selling a product that can be demonstrated, do so. Suggestions on how to conduct a demonstration are on pages 35 and 36.

Dramatization and Visual Aids

We have already identified *what* information should be communicated in the body of a presentation—the features, advantages, benefits, and proof that support the prospect's needs. This section deals with *how* to effectively communicate this information.

Prospects have many distractions and time pressures during their workday. A sales representative is competing with other sales representatives, supervisors, secretaries, emails, the telephone, meetings, deadlines, and numerous other distractions. To get and hold a prospect's interest and attention, you must use dramatization techniques and effectively engage as many of the prospect's five senses—hearing, sight, touch, taste, and smell—as possible. **Dramatization** involves communicating features, benefits, and proof in an attention-getting manner.

Engaging the Sense of Hearing

About 15 percent of all information our minds take in is through our sense of hearing. Therefore, it is important that your words, voice, and sound elements are used creatively to make your sales presentation stand out.

A sales representative should make a conscious effort to develop a new vocabulary. Every industry has its own jargon. You should learn it and use it in your sales presentation. You should also use special **power words** that will dramatize what you have to say. The prospect's name is the most powerful word you can use. Here is a list of power words to consider:

Prospect's name	Durable	Save
State-of-the-art	Proven*	New
Recommended*	Profits	Free
Up-to-date	Quality	
Cost-effective	Exciting	
Guaranteed*	Successful	
Tested, safe*	Engineered	
Labor-saving	Time-saving	
Outstanding	Improved	
Easy to use	Efficient	
Innovative	You, your	
Economical	Value	

*Excellent words for proof statements

Picture words attempt to paint visual pictures. They translate words into mental images and can dramatically improve your ability to convey features and benefits. The following are some examples:

"Our company is as solid as the Rock of Gibraltar."

"The Propulsion Plate in the sole of this running shoe is like a pole vaulter's pole that will propel the runner forward."

"The handle of this carving knife is made out of a special, indestructible polyurethane resin, which is the same material of which bowling balls are made."

"Picture yourself driving this sports car down the highway on a warm, sunny day with the top down."

Some words and phrases should be avoided. They can convey incorrect meanings, or they could intimidate or annoy the prospect. Avoid using the following:

"Sell you." Replace with "show you how you can benefit."

"Cheap." Use "inexpensive" or "requiring a small investment."

"You pay." Consider "your investment."

"Deal." Use "special offer."

"Contract" in reference to the order form. Replace with "agreement" or "paperwork."

"Sign the order." Use "approve the paperwork."

"Maybe" or "perhaps." These words suggest uncertainty.

"And-uh," "umh," "ya know," and the excessive use of "like."

So far we have discussed power words, picture words, and words to avoid during your sales presentation. While your choice of words is very important in activating the sense of hearing, how you communicate these words is equally important. Do not speak in a monotone. Vary your rate of speaking, so it is sometimes fast and at other times slow and deliberate. Vary the volume, and always speak enthusiastically.

In addition to words, you can use audio aids to engage the prospect's sense of hearing, such as an audiotape of a radio or television commercial. These can be very effective.

Silence can also be an effective tool in selling. Some sales representatives feel very uncomfortable when either they or the prospect is not talking, but silence is appropriate when you are giving the prospect time to think or reach a decision.

Engaging the Sense of Sight

About 77 percent of the information our minds take in is through our sense of sight. Therefore, your sales presentation should be primarily visual, and you should use words to reinforce the visual stimuli. Research has shown that after three days, people remembered approximately six times more information when a presentation involved both visual *and* auditory stimuli than when it involved only auditory stimuli. So, show and tell your story; do not just tell it. The following are some examples of how **visual aids** can be used to communicate benefits or offer proof.

A **portfolio** is anything listed below that can be put in a loose-leaf binder and used as visual aids during the presentation.

Create a **flip chart** of the features and benefits of the business telephone system you are selling and a list of the installation steps.

Chart or graph the week-by-week reduction of the blood pressure of executives who were participating in your health club's fitness program.

Share **print ads** from consumer magazines for your stereo receiver to prove you are conducting a heavy advertising campaign. A layout of an ad could be used if the campaign has not yet started. A **storyboard** of your television commercial could be used, too.

Bring a **product sample** of a racquetball racquet you are selling to the manager of a racquetball club.

Bring a **scale model** of a solar heating panel to demonstrate to a homeowner how effective silicone chips are in converting sunlight to heat.

Bring a **cross section** of a steel-belted radial tire to show its features to a distributor.

Provide a **list of customers** who are currently using your security surveillance systems to prove your company is large and reputable.

Provide **testimonial letters** from sales managers who have used your hotel for sales meetings and have been pleased with your services.

Display **photographs** of a homeowner's yard before and after landscaping.

Show to high school counselors a **catalog** of the university you are representing.

Provide a **brochure** of the brand of aluminum siding your firm installs.

Your travel agency offers a group tour of Europe. Show **slides** highlighting several tourist attractions that are visited by that group tour.

Play a **DVD or videotape** of your product being demonstrated.

Create a **drawing** of how new office partitions could be arranged to maximize utilization of space in an office.

Provide a **warranty or guarantee statement** for a notebook computer, indicating that your company will pay for the cost of all parts and labor for one year after purchase.

Display a **poster** of a sports celebrity who endorses your tennis shoes.

Bring an **annual report** that shows the dramatic growth in sales and profits your company has enjoyed in recent years.

Use a **scratch pad** for writing down pricing or a payout plan for your product.

Provide a **price sheet and order form.**

Share **test market data** showing that your cosmetic product captured a 25 percent share of the market.

Provide a formal **list** of the services your bank offers.

Display **point-of-sale material** used in hardware stores to promote your line of chain saws.

Provide an **article** that appeared in *Business Week* that states your company is a leader in its industry.

Some people who sell services do not use an adequate number of visual aids to make an effective presentation. They feel that since they are selling something intangible, relevant visual aids cannot be developed, so they simply tell their story. However, using visual aids is even more important when selling services than when selling tangible products, because prospects cannot actually see what they are buying. The following example will help illustrate the types of visual aids that can be used to sell a service. A salesperson for a firm such as Manpower or Kelly Services, which offers a service of temporary employees to businesses, could use the following visual aids:

Chart listing the features and benefits of hiring temporary rather than permanent workers

Graph depicting the tremendous growth in the use of temporary workers in recent years

List of customers the firm provides temporary help to in the local area

Testimonial letters from satisfied customers and temporary employees of the firm

Photographs of the exterior of the office building, executives of the firm, and temporary employees in a work setting

Brochure listing the different types of temporary employees the firm provides,

including secretaries, bookkeepers, and data-entry clerks

Annual report showing the growth in sales of the firm

Article that appeared in the local newspaper profiling the firm and its president

Formal list of the step-by-step process used to screen, train, and evaluate new temporary workers

Sample of the application form prospective temporary workers are required to complete before being hired

List of the questions used during interviews of prospective temporary employees

Description of the training the firm offers its temporary workers

Sample of the form used by supervisors to evaluate temporary workers after they have completed an assignment

Price sheet detailing the hourly rate the firm charges for different classifications of temporary workers

Contract the customer signs when hiring temporary workers

As you can see, the opportunities to use visual aids to sell a service are as numerous as those for selling a product. So show *and* tell the story about your service; do not just tell the story.

A visual aid should capture main ideas in as few words as possible, so listings rather than narratives are called for. Below are examples for Fusion that explain what profit will be realized by a retail store stocking the product. Note how much more effective the "Good Visual Aid" is at communicating information.

Poor Visual Aid

The suggested retail price per pair of Fusion shoes is $124.95. The cost to the retailer is $67.00, therefore profit of $57.95 per pair will be realized. This equates to 46.4% markup. An initial purchase of 18 pairs of Fusion will produce profit of $1,043.10.

Good Visual Aid

Retail Profit Plan Fusion Running Shoes	
Suggested retail price/pair	$ 124.95
Retailer investment/pair	67.00
Profit/pair	$ 57.95
Markup	46.4%
Recommended initial order	18 pairs
Profit/pair	$ 57.95
Total profit from this order	$1,043.10

There are some additional considerations when using visual aids. Always maintain control of each visual aid. For example, do not give the prospect your brochure to page through at his or her own pace. Place it on the prospect's desk and go through it using your finger and eye movements to direct attention where you want it. Turn pages carefully rather than flipping them, and never put a visual aid or sample back in your attaché case until you have completed the closing sequence. You may need it to handle an objection.

If you are sitting on the opposite side of the prospect's desk, you will have to be able to read printed material upside down. Be familiar with where everything is. Put paper clips on important pages so you can find them quickly. Use a colored marker to highlight important words or phrases.

In all probability, the company you are selling for has few, if any, visual aids for you to use. If this is the case, make your own. For example, develop a couple of testimonial letters, sketch something you would like photographed, or construct a graph of test data.

Perhaps the most important visual aid a salesperson has is his or her own physical appearance. A sales representative should be well groomed and dressed appropriately for the product or service being sold and for the prospect. The representative should use proper nonverbal communications such as hand gestures, facial expressions, and body positions.

Engaging the Senses of Touch, Smell, and Taste

About 8 percent of the information our minds take in is through our senses of touch, smell, and taste. While this percentage is small compared to that for our sense of sight, these senses should not be overlooked.

The sense of touch can be engaged by something as simple as shaking the prospect's hand when you greet and say good-bye. Physical touching in this socially acceptable way begins to break down the barriers between salesperson and prospect and facilitates establishing a rapport.

Another means of engaging this sense is handing something to the prospect, such as a sample of your product. Have him or her hold and examine it. People like to touch and feel things they buy. If you conduct a demonstration of how your product works, have the prospect repeat your steps in the demonstration, ensuring the prospect follows the correct steps in using your product and has a good understanding of how your product works.

The sense of smell can be engaged if you are demonstrating a food or cosmetic product. If you are discussing the fragrance of something, you should smell it first and then have the prospect smell it. Describe the fragrance using words that are as descriptive as possible. Salespeople with bad breath and body odor can engage this sense in a negative manner.

Our sense of taste is closely associated with our sense of smell. If you are doing a taste test, have a at least two samples of the product—one for you and one for the prospect. You should smell and then taste your sample while the prospect does so with the other sample. Use descriptive words that emphasize the product's features and benefits.

Conducting a Demonstration

Earlier we mentioned that a demonstration is the most effective way to dramatize features and benefits. It is effective because it allows the prospect to see the usefulness of the product. It also allows the salesperson to engage the prospect's senses of hearing, sight, touch, taste, and smell. The following are some examples of how a demonstration could be used to communicate benefits.

Product	Benefit	Demonstration
Office chair	Comfort	Ask the prospect to sit in the chair
Wine	Good taste and bouquet	Offer the prospect the opportunity to smell and taste the wine
FAX machine	Ease of installing the machine and transmitting documents	Have the prospect install the machine and transmit a document while you are instructing on what to do
Word processing software	Ease of use	Let the prospect perform some routine word processing functions
Expensive set of carving knives	Sharpness and ease of cutting	Give the prospect a fresh tomato and ask him or her to cut it

Several points should be considered when conducting a demonstration.

❏ **Plan the demonstration**—Determine what features and benefits will be communicated and what material will be needed. Consider the setting of where the demonstration will be conducted, and make sure things like electrical outlets and a table are available if needed.

❏ **Practice, practice, practice**—The best way to lose a sale is to have the demonstration not go smoothly. You do not want to fumble around or give the impression that you do not know how the product is supposed to operate.

❏ **Anticipate problems**—List all the things that could go wrong and know how to correct them.

❏ **Get the prospect physically and mentally involved.** Have him or her actively participate, and ask questions to solicit favorable comments.

❏ **Identify the prospect's needs, problems, and concerns.** Address them with your features and benefits during the demonstration.

Some products such as computers or photocopy machines require a demonstration but are too large to bring to the prospect's office. If your company has them on display in a showroom, consider asking the prospect to accompany you to the showroom. Very large products, such as stamping or robotic machines, may require you to take the prospect to a customer's place of business to see the product in operation.

Features-Benefits Worksheet

It is time to begin applying the concepts that you have learned about prospect needs, features, benefits, proof, visual aids, and dramatization. On pages 43 through 46 is a **Features-Benefits Worksheet** that will help identify the information to be communicated in the presentation. Note each form is two-sided. The worksheet provided on pages 37 through 40 is for Fusion and should be a good model for your product or service.

First, determine whether you need to complete a form for the **final user** *and* **reseller/intermediary** or just the final user. Some products require both, while others only require for the final user. The examples on page 41 will help make this determination.

You can see from the example of the Features-Benefits Worksheet for Fusion running shoes that follows requires two forms be completed—one for the final user and one for the reseller, which is a retail store. Each form

FEATURES-BENEFITS WORKSHEET—FUSION RUNNING SHOES
FINAL USER

Company You Are Selling for: <u>Brooks Shoe, Inc.</u>   Salesperson's Name: <u>Jeff Dykehouse</u>

Company You Are Selling to: <u>Taylor Sports, Inc.</u>   Product or Service You Are Selling: <u>Fusion Running Shoes</u>

Final User: <u>Men and women aged 27-54 who are serious runners</u>

Final User Problems/Needs: <u>(1) Enjoy running more, (2) Improve running performance, (3) Reduce foot, ankle,</u>

<u>and knee injuries, (4) Have greater comfort and durability, (5) Buy shoes with contemporary styling,</u>

<u>(6) Receive good value in relation to price, (7) Improve health, fitness, and sex appeal</u>

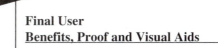

Final User Features and Advantages	Final User Benefits, Proof and Visual Aids	Corresponding Problems/Needs (Above)
1. Fusion has the exclusive silicone-filled HydroFlow dual-chamber pad in the heel of the shoes, which is visible to the consumer. Shocks from running are absorbed in the shoe, rather than the body.	Consumers get more enjoyment out of running and will be less apt to injure their feet, ankles and knees. Do a demonstration with the HydroFlow pad sample. Quote the testimonial in the ad featuring Bill Rogers, four-time winner of the New York and Boston Marathons.	#1 and 3 (above)
2. The exclusive carbon-fiber Propulsion Plate System is in Fusion. Upon impact, the energy stored in the front of the Propulsion Plate is released to propel the runner into the next stride. It offers external arch support, which provides a smooth transition from heel strike, midstance, and toe-off.	The runner's speed and endurance are enhanced. Do a demonstration using the Propulsion Plate sample. Flex the Plate to illustrate how it will provide extra lift in the step. Discuss how it works like a pole vaulter's pole and propels the runner forward. Point out that this feature resulted in winning the "Best Running Shoe" award at the Exhibition of Sports and Leisure in London. Show the rating the shoe received.	#2
3. The HydroFlow pad and Propulsion Plate were designed at the Biomechanics Evaluation Laboratory (BEL) at Michigan State University and St. Lawrence Hospital.	Consumers are guaranteed that Fusion is a state-of-the-art running shoe that will maximize performance and reduce injuries. Show BEL brochure. Point out the research and clinical activities of this laboratory.	#2 and 3
4. The upper portion of the shoe is white, gray, purple and orange and made out of nylon fabric and leather. Fusion is durable and looks attractive.	The shoe will improve sex appeal and last longer, thus saving the consumer money. Let the store manager see and feel the leather and nylon in the sample. Comment on the contemporary design.	#5, 6 and 7
5. Fusion's outer sole is made of Duralite carbon rubber compound and constructed in a webwork design. It provides better traction than other shoes and lasts longer.	Runners are less likely to fall and injure themselves on wet and icy roads. Greater durability means the consumer saves money. Let the store manager see and feel the webbed sole of the shoe.	#3, 4 and 6

Final User **Features and Advantages (Continued)**	Final User **Benefits, Proof and Visual Aids (Continued)**	**Corresponding Problems/Needs (Above)**
6. The shoe has a slip-lasted, rather than a broad-lasted, sole, which provides more flexibility.	The shoe provides greater comfort. Demonstrate the flexibility of Fusion by bending the sample.	#4
7. Fusion has a compressed molded midsole made out of Ethylene Vinyl Acetate (EVA). It acts as a cushion to absorb shock and helps the foot form to the midsole.	Running is more enjoyable and provides greater comfort. Show the store manager the cross-section of the shoe. Let him or her examine the EVA midsole.	#1 and 4
8. The shoe offers an anatomically correct fit in sizes 7 through 13. It fits better than other shoes and allows the consumer to run longer distances without foot abrasions.	Comfort, health and fitness of the runner are realized. Ask the store manager to put a pair of shoes on and walk in them to feel how well they fit.	#4 and 7
9. During production, Fusion must pass a 10-point quality inspection. The consumer is less likely to buy a defective shoe, which must be returned to the store.	The quality of the shoe is high, resulting in customer satisfaction. Show the visual aid, which explains the details of the Quality Assurance Program.	#6
10. A 30-day, money-back guarantee is offered. Defective shoes can be returned to the store for a refund.	The consumer is assured he or she will not lose money. Show the guarantee statement.	#6

FEATURES-BENEFITS WORKSHEET—FUSION RUNNING SHOES
RESELLER OR INTERMEDIARY

Reseller or Intermediary: <u>Specialty sporting goods retail store</u>

Reseller or Intermediary's Problems/Needs: <u>(1) Increase sales and profits, (2) Buy from a dependable company, which has knowledgeable, service-oriented salespeople, (3) Receive promotional discounts and advertising support, (4) Generate more store traffic, (5) Receive quick deliveries, (6) Have an opportunity to return defective merchandise for credit.</u>

Reseller or Intermediary Features and Advantages	Reseller or Intermediary Benefits, Proof and Visual Aids	Corresponding Problems/Needs (Above)
1. The suggested retail price of Fusion is $124.95, with a 46% markup. Profit per unit is $57.95.	More profit per pair of shoes will be realized than for lower-priced competitor brands. Total profit from the athletic shoe section in the store will be higher. Show price sheet and visual aid detailing the suggested retail price per unit, retailer cost, profit per unit, and markup.	#1
2. Special discounts are available for volume purchases lowering the cost to the retailer. Markup and profit per unit are higher.	Total profit from Fusion will be higher. Refer to the "Volume Program" brochure. Explain the details. Calculate the retailer's price, profit, and markup after the discounts.	#1
3. Brooks has been in the shoe business since 1914 and has been a leader in running shoe technology since 1976. The dealer is assured that Brooks is a dependable supplier.	Fusion is an innovative shoe that will appeal to the serious runner. Turnover and profits will be high. Show visual aid, which traces the history of Brooks. Discuss the series of breakthrough innovations Brooks has developed. Show the award, which indicates that the American Podiatric Medical Association endorses Fusion.	#1 and 2
4. Brooks sales representatives are experienced and experts in running shoe marketing. Retailers will get creative ideas on how to display, merchandise, and advertise Fusion.	Sales and profits from the running shoe section of the store will be maximized. Show testimonial letters from retailers who have been pleased with the support from Brooks sales representatives. Quote from the letters.	#1 and 2
5. Brooks shoes are endorsed by the world's leading runners and triathletes, including Bill Rogers, Paula Newby-Frazer, and David Scott. Consumers will see the Brooks name when the runners compete.	Consumers will seek out stores that stock Brooks shoes, resulting in greater store traffic and sales. Show the full-page ads, which include testimonials from these runners. Quote from the testimonials. Point out that the Brooks name is prominently displayed on their shirts.	#1 and 4

40

Reseller or Intermediary Features and Advantages	Reseller or Intermediary Benefits, Proof and Visual Aids	Corresponding Problems/Needs (Above)
6. A co-op advertising program is available, which reimburses the retailer 50% of the cost of print and broadcast advertising, up to 2% of net purchases. The retailer can create awareness that Fusion is available at the store.	More store traffic will be realized, and the retailer will save money in advertising expenditures. Refer the store manager to pages 2 through 5 in the "Co-op Advertising" booklet. Discuss the details.	#3 and 4
7. Fusion's introductory promotion campaign includes national advertising, point-of-sale material, display units, box-stuffers, and brochures. Consumer awareness will be created.	Store traffic, turnover, sales, and profits will be high. Show the retailer the nine-minute videotape, which will air on "Health and Fitness Today." Show the two-page ads, samples of the point-of-sale material, and photographs of the display units.	#1 and 4
8. Fusion orders can be submitted electronically to the Customer Service Department. Shipments will be received in three days. The retailer can stock less inventory.	Less money will be tied up in inventory, resulting in higher profits. Provide the URL for the Brooks Web site. Read a testimonial letter from a retailer who was pleased with Brooks's delivery schedule.	#1 and 5
9. Brooks has a liberal return policy for defective merchandise. The retailer will not lose money on defective shoes. Consumer complaints can be handled quickly.	The retailer's profits are protected and customer satisfaction is enhanced. Refer to the return goods policy in the back of the "Advanced Buyer's Guide" catalog. Read the terms to the retailer. Read a testimonial letter from a consumer who was pleased with the return policy.	#1 and 6

Product or Service Being Sold	Final User	Reseller or Intermediary
Fusion running shoes	Serious runner	Retail sporting goods store
Sales training workshop	Sales representative who needs training	Sales manager
Listing for a house with a realtor	Homeowner	None
New prescription drug	Patient	Physician
New food product	Homemaker	Supermarket
Temporary workers	Human resource manager	None
Radio advertising	Advertising manager	None
Industrial cleaning solvent	Factory maintenance manager	None

includes the problems and needs and features and benefits for the different type of prospect. If you are uncertain whether one or two forms are needed, ask your instructor.

The second step in completing your worksheet is listing the problems and needs of the final user and reseller/intermediary.

The final step in completing the worksheet is to list your features, advantages, benefits, proof, and visual aids. Review the discussion on these topics on pages 28 through 31. Be sure that for every problem/need you identify on the top part of the worksheet there are one or more corresponding features and benefits that will solve the problem or satisfy the need.

Features and benefits can be found in the areas below, which is information you gathered in Chapter 3.

❏ The industry in which your company participates

❏ Your company

❏ Your product or service

❏ Your company's distribution and delivery system

❏ Your company's promotion programs

Remember, if you are selling something that will be resold, such as a brand of golf clubs to a sporting goods store, profit is the major need and benefit for the retailer.

To complete the Features-Benefits Worksheet, remove the perforated forms on pages 43 through 46. Fill them out using a number 2 pencil so changes can be made later. Use the completed worksheet provided for Fusion on pages 37 through 40 as a guide.

FEATURES-BENEFITS WORKSHEET
FINAL USER

(Refer to pages 36 through 41 for instructions. Detach this perforated form. Fill it out in number 2 pencil. Write small.)

Company You Are Selling for: _____   Salesperson's Name: _____

Company You Are Selling to: _____   Product or Service You Are Selling: _____

Final User: *(Refer to pages 36 and 41 for clarification of final user versus resellers)*_____

Final User Problems/Needs: _____

_____

_____

_____

_____

Final User Features and Advantages	Final User Benefits, Proof and Visual Aids	Corresponding Problems/Needs (Above)

44

Final User
Features and Advantages (Continued)

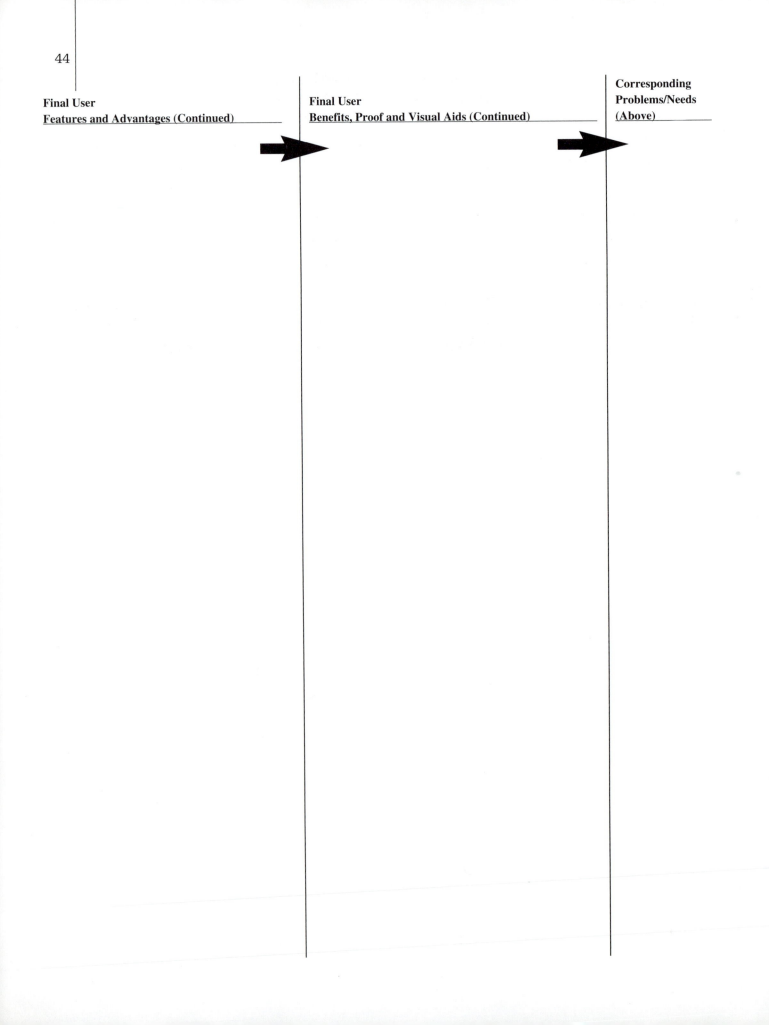

Final User
Benefits, Proof and Visual Aids (Continued)

Corresponding
Problems/Needs
(Above)

FEATURES-BENEFITS WORKSHEET
RESELLER OR INTERMEDIARY

(Refer to pages 36 through 41 for instructions. Detach this perforated form. Fill it out in number 2 pencil. Write small.)

Reseller or Intermediary: _____

Reseller or Intermediary's Problems/Needs: _____

_____

._____

_____

_____

_____

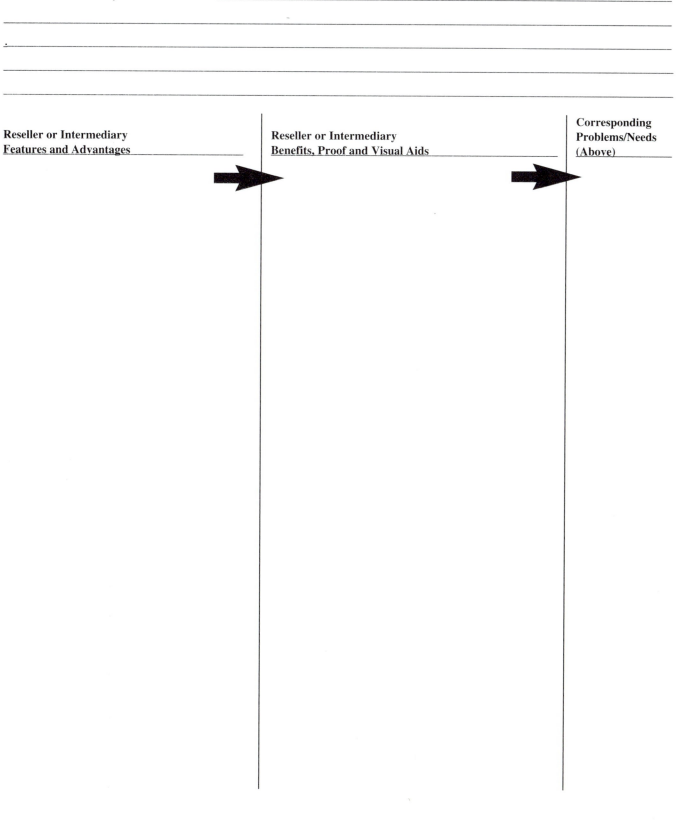

Reseller or Intermediary Features and Advantages	Reseller or Intermediary Benefits, Proof and Visual Aids	Corresponding Problems/Needs (Above)

46

Reseller or Intermediary
Features and Advantages

Reseller or Intermediary
Benefits, Proof and Visual Aids

Corresponding
Problems/Needs
(Above)

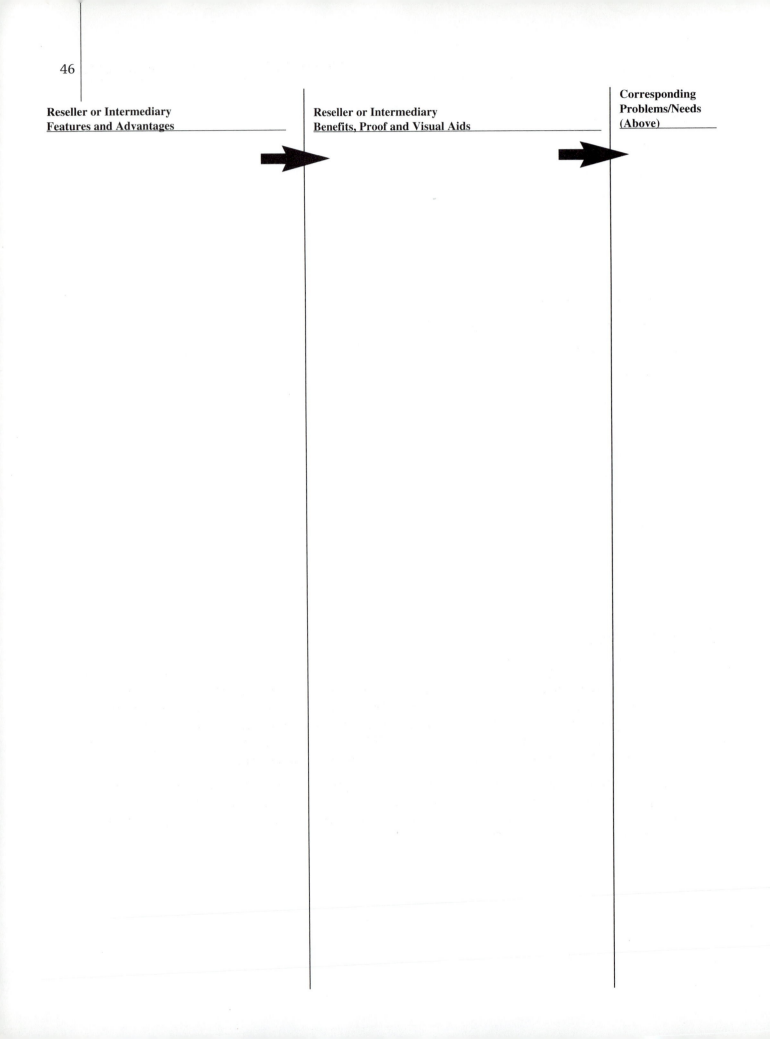

Concepts To Know

Prospect's needs

Features

Advantages

Benefits

FAB

Proof of benefits

Company-supplied proof

Independent research findings

Testimonial letters

Endorsement

Case history

Demonstration

Dramatization

Power words

Picture words

Visual aids

Features-benefits worksheet

Final user

Reseller/intermediary

Assignments

1. A Web site that features training, consulting, and articles for sales representatives is http://www.positiveresults.com. Visit the site and review the programs offered. Find an article related to this course by first selecting "Newsletter" and then "Article Archive." Develop a report on the site and what you learned from the article. If you do not find a relevant article, go to a college or public library and search databases with full-text articles on selling. ABI/Inform is an example. The librarian may have to give you a password to access databases.

2. Complete a Features-Benefits Worksheet for your presentation by following the directions on pages 36 and 41. Remove the perforated forms on pages 43 through 46. Fill it out using number 2 pencil so changes can be made later. Use the completed Fusion worksheet on pages 37 through 40 as a guide.

Chapter 6

The Approach

Objectives of the Approach

The opening of your presentation is called the **approach**. It is your first opportunity to meet the prospect face-to-face. It is the most important part of your presentation because if it is not effective, the prospect will not allow you to make a complete presentation. The first 30 seconds are the most critical because you are setting the stage for what is to follow.

When you walk into the prospect's office, he or she is typically in the middle of doing something else. You must direct attention and interest away from this activity to what you have to say. You must also establish an immediate rapport with the prospect and answer the question on every buyer's mind: "What's in this meeting for me?" Finally, you must gather information about the prospect, so you can tailor the body of the presentation around the current situation.

You should make certain assumptions concerning the prospect, which should include the following:

The Approach

1. Introduce yourself / company
2. Establish rapport
3. General benefit
4. Reason for needing information
5. Ask fact-finding questions—current situation

↓

Securing Desire

↓

Handling Objections

↓

Closing the Sale

Looking Ahead

After studying this chapter and completing the assignments, you should be able to:

1. identify appropriate questions to ask the prospect during the presentation to establish a rapport, elicit information, and determine the prospect's readiness to make a commitment,

2. practice active listening techniques,

3. describe the setting for your sales presentation, and

4. develop and effectively role play the Approach section of the sales presentation.

1. You are calling on one person, not a group, and you have never met the prospect. The prospect has never done business with your firm.

2. You called the prospect on the telephone a week ago and set up this appointment. The prospect is expecting you.

3. You were able to qualify him or her as a potential prospect. He or she is the primary decision maker and has a potential need for your product or service.

Questioning Skills

One of the most important goals of a sales presentation is to establish two-way communications with the prospect. Questions are used to solicit prospect responses.

There are many benefits to asking questions and establishing a dialogue. Since this is the first meeting with the prospect, giving the prospect an opportunity to talk by answering questions will help reduce some of the tension. These questions help you to get acquainted. Questions help keep the prospect's attention and get him or her involved in the presentation. Asking questions also shows that you are interested while helping you gather important information regarding his or her situation, problems, and needs.

There are two basic forms of questions. **Open questions** begin with "who," "what," "when," "where," "why," "which," and "how." They cannot be answered with a "yes" or "no" response. They require the prospect to explain or elaborate and thus are excellent ways to begin a dialogue or solicit information.

Whom are you buying from now?

What problems have you encountered with your current supplier?

When will you have the time to talk to the buying committee?

Where are your distribution centers located?

Why do you use this service?

Which lines are selling the best in your stores?

How often do you need quick delivery?

Closed questions, on the other hand, elicit "yes" or "no" responses. They are used to direct the flow of communication in a specific direction, to check for understanding, and to get a commitment. Closed questions begin with "is," "do," "does," "are," "can," "may," "will," "has," "have," "would," "should," and "were."

Is someone else involved in the decision making?

Does this resolve your concern about price?

Are you satisfied with the quality of service you are getting?

Can your current supplier guarantee delivery in two weeks' time?

Will delivery next week be soon enough?

Has another firm approached you about this type of service?

Would you say this is what you want?

Were you prepared to make a decision today?

You will be using open and closed questions throughout the presentation to establish a rapport with the prospect, gather facts, discover needs, confirm agreement, elicit reactions or buying signals, and close the sale. While these will be discussed in detail later, the following examples will help you better understand the questioning process in a sales presentation:

Rapport-building questions are open or closed questions that help you get acquainted with the prospect and to better understand his or her personality. "I can see from the diploma on the wall that you graduated from Sedona College. What was it like being a student there (open question)? Do you follow the sports teams (closed question)?"

Fact-finding questions solicit information about the prospect's current situation. They can be open questions such as "From whom are you currently buying?" or closed questions such as "Do you stock XYZ brand?"

Need-discovery questions are used to uncover buying motives. The following is an example of an open question: "What type of profit margin do you expect?" The following is a closed question: "Would you like to save 10 percent in your distribution costs?"

Confirming questions check for understanding or solicit agreement. They are generally closed questions such as "Can I assume you would like to solve that problem?"

Elaboration questions ask the prospect to explain something in greater detail, such as the following: "Would you tell me more?" "Could you elaborate on that point?" "I'm not sure I follow you."

Trial close questions are used to determine the prospect's readiness to buy. They measure the prospect's buying temperature. "What's your reaction to what I've said so far?" is an example.

Closing questions ask for a commitment that will allow the salesperson to achieve the sales call objective. "May we begin to provide our service to you starting next week?"

Listening Skills

Listening is a very important aspect of effective communication, but many people are poor listeners. This is partially due to the fact that people speak at a rate of 120 to 150 words per minute, while our minds can absorb 600 words per minute. It is also a result of not understanding the importance of effective listening and not knowing how to listen.

Are you a poor listener? Do you avoid eye contact when someone is speaking to you? Do you engage in physical activity or let your mind wander? Do you make judgments about what is being said before the speaker is finished? Do you nonverbally convey the impression that you are impatient or interrupt the speaker before he or she is finished? Do you give the impression that you do not care about what is being said? If you are like most people and have developed some bad listening habits, start practicing some of these techniques in your personal and professional life:

1. Maintain eye contact.

2. If you are engaged in an activity when someone begins talking to you, stop what you are doing. Listen!

3. Focus your attention on what is being said. Be alert. Also, listen for what *is not* being said. Summarize the main ideas in your mind.

4. Withhold judgment. Try to keep an open mind. Do not judge prematurely.

5. Relax and be patient with the speaker.

6. Practice active listening techniques.

Active listening involves conveying verbally and nonverbally that you are interested in and understand what the speaker is saying. Showing interest demonstrates that you think the speaker is an important person and worth listening to. Checking for understanding will ensure that your responses or future actions are appropriate. Following are some active listening techniques that you should use:

1. Periodically nod your head in agreement.

2. Tilt your head to the side as if to point your ear toward the speaker.

3. React to what is being said and encourage the speaker by saying things like "Really?", "Great", "That's interesting", "I see", "Uh-huh", "Is that so?", and "Tell me more."

4. Echo the last words the person said, such as "Your sales are up 20 percent?"

5. Paraphrase your understanding of what the speaker said. You might make a comment like, "It sounds like you're looking for . . ."

6. Ask questions related to what was said.

7. Take notes on what the person is saying.

The discussion that follows explains what to say and do during the Approach portion of your sales presentation. Be sure to use the questioning and listening techniques discussed previously in this and the other three parts of the sales presentation.

Steps in the Approach

Step 1. Introduce Yourself and Your Company

The presentation begins with an **introduction**. The first impression you make when you greet the prospect is very important. Dress appropriately for the product or service you are selling. Put your visual aids in a folder, loose-leaf binder, or attaché case. Do not put your attaché case on the prospect's desk. Keep it on your lap or on the floor. If you have a sample of your product, do not reveal it until the Securing Desire section of the presentation. When you enter the prospect's office, maintain good posture, project self-confidence, and maintain eye contact. Smile and be enthusiastic. Following is a guideline for conducting a good introduction:

1. *Greet the prospect by stating his or her name as a question.* A general rule is to use "Mr.," "Mrs.," or "Ms." and the person's last name, unless there is a clear sign that it is appropriate to use the first name. If the prospect seems to have a friendly personality and is approximately your age and of your social standing, it might be appropriate to use a first name. Be sure to pronounce the name correctly.

2. *State your name and company name* slowly and clearly so it can be understood.

3. *Shake the prospect's hand, if appropriate.* A proper handshake is one of the ways you can begin to break down some of the barriers of communication. It helps create a friendly atmosphere. You should grip the prospect's entire hand and not just the fingers. The handshake should be firm but not a "bone crusher." Men can initiate a handshake with women and women can initiate it with men. If you sense the prospect is not comfortable with a handshake, wait for him or her to initiate it.

4. *Offer your business card.* Some sales trainers recommend that the business card be given to the prospect at the end of the presentation, because it can be a distraction. The benefit to offering it here is that the prospect will feel more comfortable with this means of remembering your name and your company name. A business card for use during your role playing is provided on the inside front cover of this text. Remove it, add the information needed, and use it during role plays.

5. *Be seated.* If the prospect's demeanor and his or her office setting seem to be informal, sit in a chair as close to him or her as possible without asking for permission. If the atmosphere seems formal, ask "May I have a seat?"

Step 2. Establish a Rapport

You want to now reduce the relationship tension and create an atmosphere conducive to buying. You want to **establish a rapport** so you and the prospect can relax. Bring up something informal that does not necessarily relate to your sales call objective. Never ask, "How's business?" Many salespeople use this icebreaker, and prospects get tired of answering the same question all the time. Openings related to sports are overused, too. Try to be original and spontaneous, focusing on the prospect's interests, not yours. Remember, get him or her talking for at least two minutes. Start with open questions. Following are some examples of appropriate icebreakers:

1. *A sincere compliment.* "On my way in to see you this morning, Mr. Ryan, I noticed the attractive window display by the checkout counter. Who designs your displays for you? How do you choose which clothing to display? How has the display impacted sales?"

2. *An acquaintance.* "Mrs. Michael, the other day I was over at Apex Products, and Sue Monroe mentioned she knew you. How do you know her? Sue plays a lot of golf. Do you ever play golf with her? Tell me about the courses you play."

3. *Something you observe.* This could be something you saw in the parking lot, lobby, or buyer's office. "I can see from the pictures on the wall, Mr. Taylor, you're a sailor. What kind of a boat is that? Is it yours? How often do you get a chance to go sailing? Have you ever raced? How did you do?"

4. *Current events.* "I noticed in the paper, Mrs. Peterson, your company had its 50th anniversary last month. How did you celebrate? How many people attended? Who organized it? Was it successful?"

Let the conversation lead naturally to a conclusion and provide a transition to Step 3. For example, if you were talking about golf, you could say "I've been wanting to take up golf for some time. Perhaps I'll have a chance to try it this summer."

Step 3. State Your Purpose and General Benefit

The purpose of this step is to give the prospect an idea of where you are going and to provide a reason why he or she should listen. You should get his or her attention and arouse curiosity. The **general benefit** is a brief question or statement that reflects what the prospect will ultimately gain by listening to your presentation. It answers the prospect's question, "What's in it for me?" It has to focus on a general problem or need, because you do not know what the specific needs are yet. The following is a list of general problems or needs for businesses and consumers who buy for personal use:

General Problems and Needs For Businesses

Increase sales and profits

Reduce costs

Increase employee productivity

Improve product quality

Get better service

Save time

Improve efficiency

Reduce inventories

Improve store traffic and turnover

Improve awareness of the firm

Save the environment

Improve safety or security

Reduce employee turnover

Improve the quality of work life

General Problems and Needs For Ultimate Consumers

Save money

Increase income

Save time

Improve health and fitness

Gain prestige

Improve protection and security

Experience pride of ownership

Seek companionship

Advance in one's career

Gain approval

The general benefit should be concise—not more than one or two sentences—and just whet the prospect's appetite. It should be as specific as possible and conveyed in a dramatic way. If you are selling to a retailer or dealer, and your product will be resold, the general benefit should include a reference to profits and a benefit for the end user, such as the general benefit example for the manager of a sporting goods store that follows. The general benefit statement may be the only part of your presentation that should be memorized. The words must be chosen carefully

Prospect	General Benefit Statement
Manager of a retail sporting goods store	"Ms. Taylor, I'm here today to show you our new athletic shoe, called Fusion, which will improve the running performance of your customers, significantly reduce foot and knee injuries, and provide your store with over $1,500 in profits this spring."
Purchasing agent at a large manufacturing firm	"What I would like to do today, Dave, is show you how our new cleaning solvent will cut the amount of time it takes your people to clean the floors in your office area by 30 percent. This time savings will save you about $1,200 in the next year."
Owner of a retail store	"Mrs. Jones, how would you like to get 15 percent more advertising exposure with your target market and more traffic to your store without increasing your ad budget?"
A person in their mid-50s interested in time-sharing condominiums	"Mr. Wiley, the reason I stopped by tonight was to show you how you can buy your own condominium in beautiful Hawaii for an investment of only $35,000."
Human resource manager of a large publishing firm considering a physical fitness program for the firm's executives	"Al, I'd like to share with you some details about how you can improve the productivity and effectiveness of your top executives as much as 10 percent and reduce your medical insurance."
A business executive interested in a retirement program	"Mr. Douglas, how would you like to never worry about your financial needs during retirement?"
District sales manager, who is responsible for 30 sales representatives	"Nancy Gerts over at JGC and Associates recommended that I tell you about the workshop we offer. Her sales representatives experienced a 15 percent increase in sales after completing the course."
President of a medium-sized firm	"The banquet facilities at our hotel are perfect for your upcoming employee holiday party, Mr. Martin. I'd like to show you how we can make it a very memorable occasion, and how we can save you money, too."

and must be well organized. Above are some examples of general benefit statements:

Step 4. Explain Your Reason for Needing Information

In Step 5, you will ask the prospect several questions to learn about his or her current situation. The prospect may be reluctant to share this information unless you explain why you need it. Following are some examples of how to persuade the prospect to answer your questions:

"To find out how we can increase your profits, may I ask you a few questions?"

"Is it okay to ask you some questions about your business? That way I can recommend a program that will meet your specific needs."

Step 5. Ask Fact-Finding Questions to Determine the Prospect's Current Situation

The purpose of this step is to learn enough about the prospect so that the information you provide in the Securing Desire section will be relevant to this prospect's current situation. You are asking **fact-finding questions** to find out about the following:

1. The prospect

2. The prospect's company

3. Which of your competitors the prospect is currently doing business with, if any

4. What competitor product or service the prospect is using now.

Only ask questions that are relevant to the information you need for your presentation. At this point, do not try to identify problems or needs the prospect may have—save that for the Securing Desire section of the presentation. You should have about three to five questions. Following are examples of the fact-finding questions you would ask if you were selling Fusion shoes to a buyer at a sporting goods store and a sales training workshop to a sales manager:

Fusion Running Shoes

"How many brands of running shoes do you currently stock in your store?"

"Which brands are your most popular?" "least popular?"

"Who is your target market?"

"Are you considering any other new brands of running shoes at this time?"

Sales Training Workshop

"How many salespeople do you manage?"

"What sales training have you done in the past?"

"Who provided the training?"

"Are you considering any other sales training programs at this time?"

Notice that the questions above do not elicit responses concerning the prospect's problems or needs but rather facts concerning the current situation. Problem/need questions are offered in the Securing Desire section. The following discussion will clarify the difference.

It is important for you to understand that the fact-finding questions in the Approach are different from the **need-discovery questions** in the Securing Desire section. The example below is that of a salesperson selling health club memberships for executives to a human resource manager.

Fact-Finding Questions—Step 5 of the Approach

"How many employees work for this company?"

"How many are considered middle or upper management?"

"Do you currently have a fitness program for executives?"

"Does your company pay health insurance premiums for your executives?"

"Have you talked to any other health clubs that offer executive fitness programs?"

Need-Discovery Questions—Step 2 of Securing Desire

"What kinds of health concerns do some of your managers have, such as smoking, excessive weight, backaches, high blood pressure, or high cholesterol levels?"

"Are some of your managers under a lot of stress that may affect their performance?"

"Do you find that the health insurance premiums for your executives are increasing? If so, by how much?"

Example of the Approach

The following is an example of the Approach section of the presentation for Fusion. The "Setting the Scene" page explains the nature of the sales call. The salesperson-prospect dialogue begins on page 57.

Setting the Scene—Fusion Running Shoes

Salesperson's Name: Jeff Dykehouse

Salesperson's Company Name: Brooks Shoe, Inc.

Product or Service Being Sold: Fusion running shoes

Prospect's Name: Ms. Penny Taylor   Title: Owner/Manager

Prospect's Company Name: Taylor Sports, Inc.

Type of Business: Specialty retail sporting goods store

Prospect's Major Responsibilities: Penny manages the store and buys the athletic shoes.

Month of the Year: February

Sales Call Objective: Convince Penny to buy 18 pairs of Fusion shoes, price them at $124.95 per pair, and accept delivery by the first of next month.

Planning Guide—Fusion Approach

Salesperson-Prospect Dialogue

Step 1. Introduction

SALESPERSON: Ms. Taylor?

PROSPECT: Yes.

SALESPERSON: I'm Jeff Dykehouse with Brooks Shoe, Inc. How are you today? (Smile and be enthusiastic. Shake her hand. Present business card. Be seated.)

Step 2. Establish a rapport

SALESPERSON: I can see from the pictures on the wall that you are a runner. In what races do you compete?

PROSPECT: Last summer I ran in the Reeds Lake Run and the First National Bank Riverbank Run. I'd like to compete more often, but I just don't have the time.

SALESPERSON: I've run in the Reeds Lake Run, too. What distance do you usually run, Penny?

PROSPECT: The 5K. Anything longer than that is too hard on my body. I usually place in the top 10 or 15 in my age category.

SALESPERSON: That's great! By any chance are you going to the sporting goods show in Atlanta later this month?

PROSPECT: Not this year. My partner is going. I just can't be away from the store for four days.

SALESPERSON: I plan to be there. Maybe your partner can stop by our booth. What's his name?

PROSPECT: Bill Winston.

SALESPERSON: I'll have to talk to Bill and invite him to stop by.

Planning Guide—Fusion Approach (continued)

Salesperson-Prospect Dialogue

Step 3. Purpose and general benefit statement

SALESPERSON: Well, the reason I'm here today, Penny, is to show you our new running shoe, called Fusion. It's a technological breakthrough that will improve running performance and reduce injuries for your customers, and it will provide your store with over $1,500 in profits this spring.

Step 4. Reason for needing information

SALESPERSON: To find out how we can increase your profits, may I ask you a few questions?

PROSPECT: Okay.

Step 5. Fact-finding questions to determine the prospect's current situation

SALESPERSON: Penny, I noticed when I came in that you stock Nike, Asics, Etonic, and Reebok running shoes. How are they selling?

PROSPECT: During the running season they sell very well. Asics seems to be our top seller in the high-performance category.

SALESPERSON: Which brand would you say has the slowest turnover?

PROSPECT: I would have to say the Reebok ERS shoe. It never really caught on.

SALESPERSON: And who is your target market?

PROSPECT: Since we are a specialty sporting goods store, I would have to say we cater to the serious recreational athlete. People who shop at Wal-Mart are not the ones we're after.

SALESPERSON: Are you considering other any new high-performance running shoes at this time?

PROSPECT: The Nike rep was in last week and showed me the new 180 Air. It looks pretty good.

Preparing to Role Play

Setting the Scene and Planning Guide Form— The Approach

Now that you have learned what an effective Approach consists of, it is time to develop one for the product or service you have selected. Complete the following steps to prepare to role play the Approach.

1. Review the section on assumptions on page 50 and the rating form on page 64 to make sure you understand how the Approach should be structured and evaluated.

2. Remove the perforated forms from the text that are needed to develop and role play the Approach (pages 60, 61 and 62). Your prospect will need them when you role play.

3. Use number 2 pencil to complete the form so that changes can be made later. Number 2 pencil is recommended, because hard-lead pencils do not produce good photocopies. Print neatly so that your prospect will understand what is written.

4. Complete the Setting the Scene form, using the example for Fusion on page 56 as a guide. This will be used to orient people observing your role play.

5. Complete the two-page Planning Guide form for the Approach. Refer to the example for Fusion on pages 57 and 58. Provide a complete dialogue of what you and the prospect say, and make sure your fact-finding questions in Step 5 do not elicit prospect problems or needs.

6. Make a photocopy of the Setting the Scene and Planning Guide forms. They will be used by your prospect during the role play.

7. Before role playing the Approach, practice by reading the salesperson-prospect dialogue out loud several times.

How the Role Play Will Be Conducted

Your instructor may have you role play this portion of the sales presentation. If not, you should role play it on your own to ensure you will be properly prepared to role play the complete presentation. If possible, role play with another person who can assume the role of the prospect. The salesperson must provide a photocopy of his or her Planning Guide to the prospect. If a copy machine is not available, neatly print or type the salesperson-prospect dialogue for Steps 2 and 5 including the titles of the steps.

Your instructor will decide whether you can refer to your Planning Guide during the role play.

When you are a prospect, refer to the salesperson's Planning Guide so you know how to respond to questions. Feel free to ad lib and make up your responses to questions for which you do not have information. The only time you will object to the salesperson is when you role play Handling Objections and during the complete presentation.

The coach is the person who observes the role play. He or she fills out a rating form and critiques the salesperson at the end. When you are a coach, complete each section of the form as soon as the salesperson completes it rather than waiting until the end. After the role play, give the salesperson feedback on what skills need improvement. Here is how to get started:

1. Salesperson gives the prospect the photocopy of the completed Planning Guide form so he or she can become familiar with the responses that should be provided.

2. Salesperson sets the scene for the prospect and coach by reading the information in the Setting the Scene form on page 60.

3. Salesperson gives the coach the rating form on page 64. Space is provided to record the scores of three role plays.

4. Salesperson and prospect role play while the coach fills out the rating form.

5. Coach critiques the role play and returns the rating form to the salesperson.

To prepare for your role as salesperson, *you must rehearse the role play several times.* Say the words aloud by yourself or, better yet, to someone else.

Setting the Scene

Each time you role play, set the scene for the prospect and those observing you. Share the information that follows with them. Refer to page 56 for an example of a completed form for Fusion.

Detach this perforated form. You will need it during the role play. Print neatly in number 2 pencil so the information can be changed and photocopied.

Salesperson's Name:_____Hour:_____

Salesperson's Company Name:_____

Product or Service Being Sold:_____

Prospect's Name: *(Use role play partner's actual name)*_____ Title:_____

Prospect's Company Name:_____

Type of Business:_____

Prospect's Major Responsibilities:_____

_____

_____

_____

Month of the Year:_____

Sales Call Objective: *(Refer to page 24. Indicate the commitment you intend to secure during the presentation, not the fact that you are going to present information.)* _____

_____

_____

_____

_____

Planning Guide—The Approach

Salesperson-Prospect Dialogue

Refer to the example of the completed Planning Guide for Fusion on pages 57 and 58.

Step 1. Introduction *(Detach this perforated form. Your prospect will need it during the role play. Fill it out neatly in number 2 pencil. Write small. See page 52.)*

Step 2. Establish a rapport *(See pages 52 and 53. Keep the prospect talking for at least two minutes. Record what is said for both sides of the conversation.)*

(continued)

Planning Guide—The Approach (continued)

Salesperson-Prospect Dialogue

Step 3. Purpose and general benefit statement *(See pages 53 and 54. What is in it for the prospect?)*

Step 4. Reason for needing information *(See page 54.)*

Step 5. Fact-finding questions to determine the prospect's current situation *(These should be fact-finding questions, not ones related to the prospect's needs or problems. See pages 54 and 55.)*

You must get used to hearing yourself play the role. Study the Planning Guide, rehearse the role play, then study the guide again so you can see what areas need improvement. Record yourself with a tape recorder several times to hear what you sound like. Use the rating form on page 64 to evaluate yourself.

Materials Needed to Role Play the Approach

You will need your completed Setting the Scene form on page 60, two-page Planning Guide, a photocopy of the two-page Planning Guide for the prospect, Approach Rating Form on page 64, business card, and this textbook. If you do not have access to a photocopy machine to reproduce your Planning Guide for the prospect, neatly print or type the salesperson-prospect dialogue for Steps 2 and 5, including the titles of the steps.

Concepts To Know

Approach

Open questions

Closed questions

Rapport-building questions

Fact-finding questions

Need-discovery questions

Confirming questions

Elaboration questions

Trial close questions

Closing questions

Active listening

Introduction (in the presentation)

Establish a rapport

General benefit

Assignments

1. A Web site that offers an electronic newsletter for sales professionals is http://www.salesdog.com. Visit the site and find an article from back issues that is related to this course. Develop a report on the site and what you learned in the article. If you do not find a relevant article, go to a college or public library and search databases with full-text articles on selling. ABI/Inform is an example. The librarian may have to give you a password to gain access to the databases.

2. Complete the Setting the Scene and Approach Planning Guide forms for your presentation by following the directions on pages 59 and 63. Remove the perforated forms on pages 60 through 62. Fill them out using number 2 pencil so changes can be made later. Use the completed forms for Fusion on pages 56 through 58 as guides.

3. Prepare to role play the Approach. Follow the instructions on pages 59 and 63.

Approach Rating Form (25 Points)

Salesperson's Company: _____   Hour: _____

Product/Service: _____   Salesperson's Name: _____

	Possible Score	Actual Score Record Scores of Three Role Plays		
Prospect's Company: _____				
–Ability in introducing yourself and company	2	_____	_____	_____
–Ability in offering a firm handshake, presenting your business card, and being seated	2	_____	_____	_____
–Ability in establishing a rapport by asking questions and getting the prospect to respond; ability in keeping the prospect talking long enough to feel relaxed	5	_____	_____	_____
–Ability in stating your purpose and general benefit	5	_____	_____	_____
–Ability in explaining your reason for needing information	2	_____	_____	_____
–Ability in asking appropriate fact-finding questions to determine the prospect's current situation	5	_____	_____	_____
–Ability in being enthusiastic, smiling, and using the prospect's name	4	_____	_____	_____
Total	25 pts.	_____	_____	_____

Coach's notes and comments:

Chapter 7

Securing Desire

Objectives of Securing Desire

The objective of the Securing Desire section of your presentation is to persuade your prospect to want to buy your product or service. Since you are to assume he or she has never done business with your firm, you must first provide some information about the firm. Then you will discover the prospect's problems and needs, while providing the benefits of your product or service and of doing business with you and your company. When the prospect seems skeptical, you will offer proof of the benefits. Appropriate words and visual and audio aids will be used to dramatize the benefits. These were discussed in Chapter 5 on pages 31 through 36.

Below are the steps in Securing Desire.

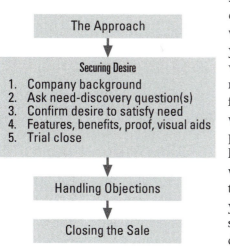

The Approach

Securing Desire
1. Company background
2. Ask need-discovery question(s)
3. Confirm desire to satisfy need
4. Features, benefits, proof, visual aids
5. Trial close

Handling Objections

Closing the Sale

Steps in Securing Desire

Step 1. Familiarize the Prospect with Your Company

Since you are assuming the prospect has never done business with your company, you must provide him or her with an overview of the company and explain why

Looking Ahead

After studying this chapter and completing the assignments, you should be able to:

1. *elicit problems and needs of the prospect,*

2. *identify and communicate features, benefits, and proof that appeal to the prospect's problems and needs, and*

3. *develop and effectively role play the Securing Desire section of the presentation including the extensive use of visual aids.*

it is uniquely qualified to serve the prospect's needs. Begin by asking what the prospect already knows about your company. Then provide the following information:

1. *A brief history of the firm*—Give a brief description about when your company was founded and by whom. If photographs of the original building or founders are available, share them with the prospect. Discuss how the company has changed.

2. *Major achievements in recent years*—These might include the introduction of innovative products or services, awards the company received, acquisitions, or expansions. Show the prospect a chronological list of these achievements.

3. *Size in terms of sales, number of employees, or number of branches*—If your firm is an industry leader, convey this to the prospect. People like to do business with large, reputable firms with a proven track record. Show the prospect a copy of your firm's annual report and discuss its growth in sales. If your firm is small, stress the benefits of being small, such as personalized service and quick response to customer requests. Provide photographs of the executives accompanied by a brief biography of each. Discuss the experience of these executives.

4. *Types of products or services you offer*—Show the prospect a brochure or typed list of the broad range of products or services you offer.

5. *List of current customers*—Be sure to include large firms that buy from you and, ideally, those that compete directly or indirectly with the prospect.

The purpose of familiarizing the prospect with your company is to establish the credibility of your firm and to convince the prospect that doing business with your company is worthwhile. This discussion should be about two minutes in length and include three or four visual aids.

Step 2. Ask Need-Discovery Questions Until You Identify One Specific Problem

In Step 5 of the Approach, you asked **fact-finding questions** to determine the prospect's current situation. Now you must continue to question the prospect until one problem or need is identified. You will recall that problems or needs are gaps between the prospect's current situation and the ideal situation. **Need-discovery questions** should allow you to diagnose the prospect, just as a doctor diagnoses patients; identify the ailment. Guide the prospect through the use of questions and identify a problem or need. Identifying these problems is the most challenging part of Securing Desire. Start with general, open-ended questions, like the following, to see if the prospect has any problems in mind.

"What problems have you been having?"

"How would you describe the ideal situation?"

"Exactly what are you looking for?"

If the prospect offers some problems, ask him or her to elaborate on them. Find out all the details.

"Tell me more."

"Could you elaborate on that point?"

"What do you mean by _____?"

Often, the prospect does not have a clear understanding of problems or needs. In this case, offer some specific ones with closed questions.

"Do you ever have any complaints about _____?"

"Have you experienced problems in the area of _____?"

"Are you totally satisfied with _____?"

"Does _____ meet all of your needs?"

"Is _____ a concern of yours?"

Refer to your completed Features-Benefits Worksheet in Chapter 5 on pages 43 through 46.

The problems and needs that could be addressed should be noted on the top portion of the form on pages 43 and 45.

The first problem/need you identify must be one that provides an opportunity to discuss the most important features and benefits of your product or service. You must show your product or explain the details of your service. After the prospect fully understands what is being sold, other needs can then be exploited.

The examples that follow illustrate features and benefits related to three problems/needs for different products and services. Notice that, in each case, the first one allows the salesperson to show the product or explain the details of the service.

Questions to determine all of the prospect's problems/needs should not be asked one after another. Ask questions to identify *one* problem/need and support it with features, benefits, and proof. Then ask additional questions to identify a *second* problem/need and support it with features, benefits, and proof.

Step 3. Confirm the Prospect's Desire to Solve the Problem or Satisfy the Need

At this point, a **confirming question** is used to "pin the prospect down" and get him or her to agree that there is a problem or need. If you cannot get the prospect to agree to this, nothing will be bought. Do not ask for a commitment related to your sales call objective.

Product or service being sold	Identify problems/needs related to the . . .
Running shoe sold to a manager of a retail sporting goods store (Fusion)	1. features and benefits of the running shoe 2. details of the advertising and promotional program 3. profits the retailer will enjoy
Industrial cleaning solvent sold to a manufacturing firm	1. chemical composition of the product and why it cleans floors so well 2. ease of application and use 3. savings of time and money to clean floors
Hotel meeting rooms sold to a sales manager planning a training program for sales representatives	1. size of the meeting rooms, seating arrangements, and audiovisual equipment available 2. variety and quality of the food served to guests 3. overnight guest rooms and accommodations
Radio station advertising time sold to a local retailer	1. type of music, news, weather, and sports programming 2. efficiency of the station in reaching the retailer's target audience 3. capabilities of station personnel to write and produce a radio commercial for the retailer

Confirmation is related to the problem or need, not in buying.

To confirm the prospect's desire, the following types of questions can be asked:

"Then you're looking for _____?"

"So you need a way to _____?"

"Can I assume a solution to that problem would be of interest to you?"

"You want _____?"

"Is solving that problem a concern of yours?"

"Then, you need _____?"

Step 4. Provide Features, Benefits, and Proof That Will Solve the Problem or Satisfy the Need—Use Visual Aids and Dramatization

Step 3 got the prospect to agree there was a problem/need. Step 4 must show the prospect that (1) he or she has a need for the *type* of product/service you are offering, (2) your specific *brand* of product will meet these needs, (3) your *company* is worth doing business with, (4) your *price* is right, and (5) now is the *time* to commit.

The information used to convince the prospect that you can solve a problem or satisfy a need consists of the features, advantages, benefits, and proof noted in your Features-Benefits Worksheet that was completed in Chapter 5. Visual aids and dramatization are necessary in communicating this information effectively. Engage the prospect's senses of sight, hearing, touch, smell, and taste where appropriate. If you are selling a product, a demonstration may be called for. Refer to your Worksheet and discussion on pages 28 through 36 in Chapter 5 for clarification.

The issue of whether you should mention competitor products or services when you are discussing features and benefits is controversial. It is usually best not to mention competitors unless the prospect brings it up or unless it is absolutely necessary. If you do mention them, be professional. Do not speak disparagingly about competitors. Rather, you might show how their products are good but how yours are better.

Step 5. Offer a Trial Close

You will learn in Chapter 9, on Closing the Sale, that you should close when the prospect is ready to close. This may be before you have presented all your benefits. To determine whether the prospect is ready to close, you must frequently ask questions to get a reaction or opinion on something you have said. These are called **trial closes**, and they give the prospect an opportunity to give you a buying signal. Trial closes consist of opinion-seeking questions, not order-asking questions. These questions test the prospect's readiness to buy. They are designed to measure the prospect's buying temperature: "cold," "warm," or "hot." Ask trial close questions after presenting important benefits or after attempting to resolve an objection. If the answer to your question is positive, you may wish to ask a closing question and close the sale. The exhibit of the thermometer on page 70 illustrates when to close the sale. Following are some examples of trial closes you can use in Securing Desire:

"What's your reaction to what I've said so far?"

"How does that sound?"

"What do you think?"

"Are we together on this?"

"Interesting, isn't it?"

"You *would* like to (state benefit), wouldn't you?"

"Is this what you're looking for?"

"In your opinion, do you feel this is an important benefit?"

"How does that strike you?"

"Does that make sense?"

"Am I on the right track?"

"Are we in agreement so far?"

Step 6. Close or Repeat Steps 2 through 5

After the trial close, if you sense the prospect is ready to buy, ask for the commitment. In other words, **close the sale**. If the buying temperature

For the athlete who understands the physical benefits of performance engineered equipment and demands state-of-the-art technology. For the athlete ". . .who wants a 'do everything' shoe . . ."[1]

Construction
• Slip-lasted

Outsole
• Clear silicone rubber
• State-of-the-art high abrasion rubber webwork design

Midsole
• Tri-density compression molded EVA
• Propulsion Plate™ system with full length carbon fiber contour plate offers exceptional stability, cushioning and performance for efficiency of push off during the forward phase of running
• Rearfoot HydroFlow® custom cushioning
• Modified diagonal rollbar
• Forefoot visco-elastic pad
• TPR heel counter
• Combination of midsole componentry produces a system that doesn't break down or bottom out

Upper
• Ventilated nylon mesh and teijin
• Reflective trim
• Speed lacing system
• HydroTech sockliner for moisture-wicking and cushioning

4870 Men's • Purple/Orange/White • Sizes 5-12,13
3598 Women's • Purple/Orange/White • Sizes 6-10,11

The Fusion is a training shoe which incorporates a full length contour Propulsion Plate offering exceptional stability, cushioning, and performance.

The contour propulsion plate is designed to achieve a specific spring quality for the activity of running. Carbon fiber is an elastic material possessing great strength and durability, but is extremely lightweight.

The contour propulsion plate incorporates a rearfoot stability component, an external arch support, and a forefoot propulsion component. The external arch provides exceptional stability while at the same time storing energy during foot pronation. The propulsion component of the plate design assists the foot in providing more efficient push off.

[1]Reprinted with permission from *American Athletics Magazine*, Fall/Winter 1990, "The Six Best New Shoes" by Gary Goettelmann. For subscription information: 1 year $17.95, P.O. Box 1499, Los Altos, CA 94040.

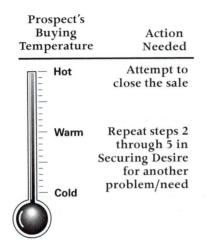

Prospect's Buying Temperature	Action Needed
Hot	Attempt to close the sale
Warm	Repeat steps 2 through 5 in Securing Desire for another problem/need
Cold	

is warm or cold, repeat Steps 2, 3, 4, and 5. Identify another problem; confirm the desire to solve the problem; provide features, benefits, and proof; then ask another trial close question. Refer to the diagram on the inside front cover. Notice the arrows that show how to recycle the steps in Securing Desire or proceed to Closing the Sale.

Example of Securing Desire

The following dialogue is an example of the Securing Desire section of the presentation for Fusion. It begins where the Approach section left off. Recall that Jeff Dykehouse is conducting a presentation with Penny Taylor, the manager of a sporting goods store. Review the Fusion example beginning on page 56 before you read the next section.

PLANNING GUIDE—FUSION SECURING DESIRE

Salesperson-Prospect Dialogue

Step 1. Familiarize the prospect with information about your company he or she does not already have.

SALESPERSON: Penny, do you know very much about Brooks?

PROSPECT: Not really. I know Brooks has been around for a long time, and I've seen some of your ads in <u>Runner's World</u>.

SALESPERSON: Brooks got started back in 1914, so we have been in the shoe business for a long time. In 1972, we began to produce our own brand of athletic shoes. Our corporate headquarters are located in Rockford, Michigan.

While we concentrate our efforts on running and walking shoes, we offer a full line of athletic shoes. (Show "Footwear Catalog." Point out the categories of shoes offered by Brooks.)

Brooks is the official shoe company for the Ironman World Triathlon Championships in Hawaii and the Coors Lite Biathlon series. Also, we have the only running shoe technology that is endorsed by the American Podiatric Medical Association. (Show certificate that verifies this endorsement.)

Our line is very well established in the west Michigan area. (Show the list of customers, mentioning a few.)

Pretty impressive isn't it?

PROSPECT: Yes it is.

SALESPERSON: We offer high-quality products that will provide handsome profits for your store, Penny.

PLANNING GUIDE—FUSION SECURING DESIRE
(continued)

Salesperson-Prospect Dialogue

Step 2. Question(s) to identify *first* problem/need

SALESPERSON: What would you say your customers look for in the running shoes they buy?

PROSPECT: A shoe has to look good, but most of my customers are looking for a shoe that will provide better performance and reduce injuries.

Step 3. Question to confirm prospect's desire to solve problem or satisfy first need

SALESPERSON: So your customers look for these features in the running shoes they buy?

PROSPECT: Yes.

Step 4. Features/benefits/proof to support first problem/need. Use visual aids and dramatization.

SALESPERSON: Penny, here it is. (Show sample. Get reaction.) Fusion is the most technologically advanced shoe in the industry. What makes it so unique is the carbon fiber Propulsion Plate System in the midsole. (Give Penny the Propulsion Plate sample.) The way it works is, upon impact, the energy stored in the front of the Plate is released to propel the runner into the next stride. (Do a demonstration with the Plate.) It acts like a pole-vaulter's pole. The energy stored in the pole propels the vaulter over the bar. The shoe's structure allows it to similarly store energy. The benefit is that the runner's speed and endurance are enhanced.

Fusion also contains the patented HydroFlow pad in the heel of the shoe. (Show example.) The tremendous impact on the foot while running cushions like a shock absorber. (Do a demonstration.) This will help reduce foot injuries.

Both of these technologies were developed by the Biomechanics Evaluation Laboratory at Michigan State University. (Show B.E.L. brochure. Discuss research activities.) Fusion is available in men's and women's sizes.

Step 5. Trial close

SALESPERSON: What do you think, Penny?

PROSPECT: It sounds good so far.

PLANNING GUIDE—FUSION SECURING DESIRE
(continued)

Salesperson-Prospect Dialogue

Step 2. Question(s) to identify *second* problem/need

> SALESPERSON: This is a relatively new store, Penny. Are you satisfied with the amount of traffic you are getting?

> PROSPECT: We had a good holiday season, but it is dead right now. You know what Michigan winters are like.

Step 3. Question to confirm prospect's desire to solve problem or satisfy second need

> SALESPERSON: So you need a way to get more shoppers in your store?

> PROSPECT: That would be nice.

Step 4. Features/benefits/proof to support second problem/need. Use visual aids and dramatization.

> SALESPERSON: We have developed an extensive promotional campaign for Fusion that will create awareness of the product in your trading area and bring customers into your store.
>
> Our four-color, two-page spreads will begin in the April editions of <u>Runner's World</u> and <u>Running Times.</u> The ads will also appear in <u>Michigan Runner.</u> (Show samples of ads.) We produced a nine-minute videotape that will air on the "Health and Fitness Today" show. We also have an excellent co-op advertising program. (Show "Co-op Advertising Planner" booklet. Discuss details.)
>
> At the point of sale there are display units, posters, and brochures available that tie in with our advertising. (Show samples.)
>
> Finally, we have world-class athletes, such as runners like Bill Rogers, triathletes like Paula Newby-Fraser and Dave Scott, who will be endorsing the Brooks line this season. (Quote from the ads that feature testimonials from these runners.)

Step 5. Trial close

> SALESPERSON: How does that sound?

> PROSPECT: It's pretty impressive.

PLANNING GUIDE—FUSION SECURING DESIRE
(continued)

Salesperson-Prospect Dialogue

Step 2. Question(s) to identify *third* problem/need

SALESPERSON: This is a beautiful store in a prime location. Your overhead must be pretty high. Penny, do you find it more and more difficult to turn a profit?

PROSPECT: That's an understatement!

Step 3. Question to confirm prospect's desire to solve third problem or satisfy third need

SALESPERSON: Then you want to maximize your profit margin and profit per unit on your running shoes?

PROSPECT: Isn't that what being in business is all about?

Step 4. Features/benefits/proof to support third problem/need. Use visual aids and dramatization.

SALESPERSON: Take a look at our profit schedule on Fusion. I think you'll be impressed. (Show visual aid that details pricing and profit.)

As you can see, our suggested retail price on Fusion is $124.95. Your investment is $67.00 per pair so you make $57.95 profit on each unit sold. That's 46 percent markup!

Now, if you turn only four pairs per week, that's $231.80 in profit. If you compare this to the profit you make on an $80 shoe, we're 60 percent higher. With our heavy advertising, you could easily turn 30 to 40 pairs this season. That would mean $1,500 to $2,000 profit just on Fusion!

Step 5. Trial close

SALESPERSON: Is this the kind of profit you're looking for, Penny?

PROSPECT: Yes, it is in line with our expectations.

Preparing to Role Play

Planning Guide Form—Securing Desire

Now that you have learned what an effective Securing Desire section of the presentation consists of, it is time to develop one for the product or service you have selected. Complete the following steps to prepare to role play Securing Desire.

1. Refer to your completed Features-Benefits Worksheet on pages 43 through 46. The problem/needs, features, benefits, proof, visual aids, and dramatization needed for Securing Desire are in the worksheet. Also review the rating form on page 81 to make sure you understand how the role play of Securing Desire will be evaluated.

2. Detach the perforated form from the text for the Securing Desire section (pages 76 through 79). Your prospect will need it when you role play

3. Use a number 2 pencil to complete the form so that changes can be made later. Number 2 pencils are recommended because hard-lead pencils do not produce good photocopies. Print neatly so that your prospect will understand what is written.

4. Complete the Planning Guide form for Securing Desire that identifies three problem/needs. Refer to the example for Fusion on pages 71 through 74. Provide a complete dialogue of what you and the prospect say. Make sure to incorporate extensive visual aids to communicate features and benefits.

5. Make a photocopy of the completed Planning Guide form.

6. Practice Securing Desire by reading the salesperson/prospect dialogue several times out loud.

How the Role Play Will Be Conducted

Your instructor may have you role play Securing Desire. If not, you can role play it on your own or get two other people to participate. Review the instructions in the section "How the Role Play Will Be Conducted" on pages 59 and 63. This also applies to role playing Securing Desire. You will not role play the Approach. Assuming you have just completed the Approach, you will be seated when you begin. Do not try to close the sale. The prospect should not offer any objections during this role play.

Materials Needed to Role Play Securing Desire

You will need your completed Setting the Scene form on page 60, Planning Guide for Securing Desire, a photocopy of the Planning Guide for the prospect, Securing Desire Rating Form, product samples, visual and audio aids, and text to successfully role play Securing Desire. If you are going to do a demonstration of your product, you will need the appropriate materials. If you do not have access to a photocopy machine to reproduce your Planning Guide for the prospect, make a typed or handwritten copy of the salesperson-prospect dialogue for Step 2 for each problem/need, including the title of the step.

PLANNING GUIDE—SECURING DESIRE

Salesperson-Prospect Dialogue

Refer to the example of the completed Planning Guide on pages 71 through 74 and your Features-Benefits Worksheet on pages 43 through 46.

Step 1. Familiarize the prospect with information about your company he or she does not already have. *(Detach this perforated form. Your prospect will need it when you role play. Fill it out neatly in number 2 pencil. See pages 65 and 66. Use the prospect's name throughout.)*

PLANNING GUIDE—SECURING DESIRE
(continued)

Salesperson-Prospect Dialogue

Step 2. Question(s) to identify *first* problem/need *(The first need should allow you to discuss the most important benefits your product or service has to offer. Also, show your product or explain your service. See pages 66 and 67.)*

Step 3. Question to confirm prospect's desire to solve problem or satisfy first need *(See pages 67 and 68.)*

Step 4. Features/benefits/proof to support first problem/need. Use visual aids and dramatization. *Refer to your Features-Benefits Worksheet on pages 43 through 46. Also see page 68.)*

Step 5. Trial close *(See page 68.)*

PLANNING GUIDE—SECURING DESIRE
(continued)

Salesperson-Prospect Dialogue

Step 2. Question(s) to identify *second* problem/need

Step 3. Question to confirm prospect's desire to solve problem or satisfy second need

Step 4. Features/benefits/proof to support second problem/need. Use visual aids and dramatization.

Step 5. Trial close *(Use a different trial close than for the first problem/need.)*

PLANNING GUIDE—SECURING DESIRE
(continued)

Salesperson-Prospect Dialogue

Step 2. Question(s) to identify *third* problem/need

Step 3. Question to confirm prospect's desire to solve third problem or satisfy third need

.

Step 4. Features/benefits/proof to support third problem/need. Use visual aids and dramatization.

Step 5. Trial close *(Use a different trial close than for the first two problem/needs.)*

.

(Prospect: At some point during the Securing Desire section of the presentation, you should ask about the price of the product or service.)

Concepts to Know

Review from Chapter 5

    Prospect's needs

    Features

    Advantages

    Benefits

    Proof of benefits

    Company-supplied proof

    Independent research findings

    Testimonial letters

    Endorsement

    Case history

    Demonstration

    Dramatization

    Visual aids

    Features-benefits worksheet

Review from Chapter 6

    Fact-finding questions

    Need-discovery questions

New concepts—Chapter 7

    Confirming question

    Trial close

    Closing the sale

Assignments

1. A Web site that offers training for salespeople is http://www.salesvault.com. Visit the site and review the services offered. Find an article related to this course by selecting "Sales Articles" at the top of the home page. Develop a report on the site and what you learned from the article. If you do not find a relevant article, go to a college or public library and search databases with full-text articles on selling. ABI/Inform is an example. The librarian may have to give you a password to access to the databases.

2. Complete the Securing Desire section of your presentation by following the directions on page 75. Detach the perforated Planning Guide form on pages 76 through 79. Fill it out using a number 2 pencil so changes can be made later. Use the completed form for Fusion on pages 71 through 74 as a guide. The Features-Benefits Worksheet you completed in Chapter 5 should have most of the information needed for the Planning Guide in this chapter. Use visual aids extensively. Prepare typed visual aids where they are needed.

3. Prepare to role play Securing Desire. Follow the instructions on page 75.

Securing Desire Rating Form (25 Points)

Salesperson's Company: _____   Hour: _____

Product/Service: _____   Salesperson's Name: _____

	Possible Score	Actual Score		
Prospect's Company: _____		**Record Scores of Three Role Plays**		
–Ability in briefly familiarizing the prospect with your company	4	_____	_____	_____
–Ability in asking questions and clearly identifying problems/needs	3	_____	_____	_____
–Ability in confirming the prospect's desire to solve each problem or satisfy each need	2	_____	_____	_____
–Ability in providing features and benefits relevant to each problem/need	5	_____	_____	_____
–Ability in offering proof, including a demonstration, if appropriate	3	_____	_____	_____
–Ability in offering a trial close after each benefit statement	2	_____	_____	_____
–Ability in incorporating visual (and/or audio) aids, if appropriate, into the presentation, putting them in front of the prospect, and maintaining control of them	3	_____	_____	_____
–Ability in being enthusiastic, smiling, and using the the prospect's name	3	_____	_____	_____
Total	25 pts.	_____	_____	_____

Coach's notes and comments:

Chapter 8

Handling Objections

Goals of Handling Objections

In most cases when a salesperson tries to close the sale, the prospect has one or more reasons for not wanting to offer a commitment. Overcoming this resistance to achieve the sales call objective is called **Handling Objections**. The prospect needs more justification (benefits) and reassurance (proof) before he or she can make a buying decision.

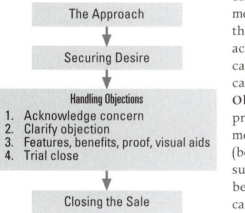

The Approach

↓

Securing Desire

↓

Handling Objections
1. Acknowledge concern
2. Clarify objection
3. Features, benefits, proof, visual aids
4. Trial close

↓

Closing the Sale

Looking Ahead

After studying this chapter and completing the assignments, you should be able to:

1. anticipate resistance (objections) that will be offered by prospects,

2. identify features, benefits, and proof that will overcome resistance, and

3. develop and effectively role play the Handling Objectives section of the sales presentation, including the extensive use of visual aids.

Preparing to Handle Objections

Anticipating Objections

Throughout this text, the importance of being a prepared salesperson has been stressed. This need to be prepared applies especially to the area of Handling Objections. A salesperson must anticipate the prospect's objections and determine ahead of time what benefits will resolve each objection.

No purchase is ever made—whether it is a $.75 candy bar or a $25,000 automobile—unless the prospect says "yes" to the following five questions, called the **Five Buying Decisions:**

Question 1. "Do I *need* any brand in a product or service category?" (e.g., a new car)

Question 2. "Will this specific brand of *product or service* satisfy my needs or solve my problems?" (e.g., a Honda Accord)

Question 3. "Is this *source* (company and sales representative) the one from whom I should buy?" (e.g., a specific Honda dealership)

Question 4. "Is the *price* right/*money* available?" (e.g., the sticker price, rebates, trade-in allowance, financing, and leasing)

Question 5. "Is the *time* to buy now or should I wait to buy?"

The salesperson must obtain five affirmative responses before the prospect will buy.

This concept is useful when anticipating objections, because all objections can be classified under one of the Five Buying Decisions. The following are examples of objections for Fusion, which is being sold to a retailer; a cellular telephone, which is being sold to a service manager; and a sales training workshop, which is being offered to a sales manager. Note that all the objections are classified as need, product/service, source, price/money, or time objections. Also, note that they are declarative statements of the reasons the prospect does not want to buy. Make sure the objections you identify are declarative statements, not questions that request more information (e.g., "I like the product we use now," rather than "Can you tell me more about your product?")

Objections for Fusion Running Shoes

Need Objections

"We already stock four brands of running shoes."

"I don't have any room on the shelf for another line."

"We have too much inventory of the brands we stock now."

Product/Service Objections

"I think the cushion sole of the Nike 180 Air shoe is better than the Propulsion Plate system in your shoe."

"Personally, I prefer the styling of the Nike 180 Air."

Source Objections *(objections related to doing business with the salesperson or the salesperson's company)*

"Your company isn't spending enough money in advertising to promote this shoe."

"Brooks is a small company compared to Nike and Reebok."

"I like the salesperson from Nike. He has some good merchandising ideas and accepts returns on defective shoes."

"Nike ships our orders within two days."

Price/Money Objections

"Your suggested retail price of $124.95 is too high. People won't pay that much for a running shoe."

"I don't have the money to tie up in another line."

"Your shoe doesn't have a proven track record. I don't think the turnover and profit will be adequate."

Time Objections *(objections related to allowing the salesperson to achieve the sales call objective during this sales call)*

"I want to postpone a decision until next month."

"There is still snow on the ground. People won't buy running shoes until spring."

"Give me a call in April. I'll consider Fusion then."

Objections for a Cellular Phone

Need Objections

"Our technicians can use pagers and customers' phones when they are out making service calls."

"Calls can be made in the morning before our technicians leave the office or in the late afternoon when they return."

Product/Service Objections

"If our technicians use the phone while driving, they may be more apt to have an accident."

"The other model we are looking at has more features."

"Yours only has a two-year warranty."

Source Objections

"We're negotiating with another cell phone company."

"Your company doesn't have its own service department."

"The last salesperson from your company who called on us was a real jerk."

Price/Money Objections

"The price of your phone is 15 percent higher than the other one we are considering."

"The cost of each call on a cellular phone is very high."

"The other company we are talking to has 60-day dating terms."

Time Objections

"Call me back in a week or so."

"I have to get approval from my boss."

Objections for a Two-Day Sales Training Workshop

Need Objections

"I don't need your workshop because my salespeople are already well trained."

"I conducted some training about one year ago."

"All my salespeople have at least five years of experience and are college graduates."

Product/Service Objections

"We think on-the-job training is better."

"Your workshop isn't appropriate for experienced salespeople."

"I think a one-day workshop would be adequate."

Source Objections

"I have never heard of your consulting firm."

"Your workshop leader doesn't have any experience selling the types of products we offer."

"Most of your former clients are manufacturing firms. We are a distributor."

Price/Money Objections

"Your price of $490 for each participant is too high."

"I'll lose money during the two days my salespeople are in the workshop and not out selling."

Time Objections

(same objections as for the previous cellular phone example)

The way to prevent objections is to anticipate them and then build benefits that will resolve each objection into the Securing Desire section of your presentation.

How to Resolve Need, Product/Service, and Source Objections

The information needed to resolve objections consists of features, benefits, and proof, which are inherent in your industry, company, product or service, price, distribution system, and promotional programs. Many of the benefits you will need to resolve objections are listed in your Features-Benefits Worksheet on pages 43 through 46.

Need objections are ones related to buying *any product or service* offered by your industry rather than your specific brand of product or type of service. To overcome these objections, provide features and benefits to the prospect that show the consequences of not buying. For example, a cellular phone salesperson might discuss how a cell phone can save time, improve productivity, and improve customer relations.

Product or service objections are those associated with buying *your model of product or type of service*. Resolve these objections by discussing the special features and benefits of the product. Explain how it is made, of what it is made, and how it can be used. Discuss workmanship, durability, and quality. Depending on what you are selling, it might be appropriate to discuss how the product will save time or money. If you are selling a service, provide features and benefits of each aspect of the service and explain why your company's employees are qualified to provide superior service.

Source objections deal with resistance to *doing business with your company or with you personally*. Provide features and benefits that show your firm is reputable and is worthwhile to do business with. Case histories or testimonial letters from satisfied customers can be very effective. Occasionally, salespeople get source objections because prospects want to continue to buy from competitor salespeople. Overcome these objections by talking about your formal education, training, expertise, and successes with other customers.

How to Resolve Price/Money Objections

The objections that seem to challenge salespeople the most are **price/money objections**. It is one area in which the prospect can make a quantitative comparison between two competing products or services. However, prospects rarely buy based on price alone. If a salesperson anticipates price/money objections and develops means to resolve them before the sales call, these objectives can be overcome. Following are some methods to consider when handling price/money objections.

1. Build up the *value* of the product or service—The perceived value of a product is a function of the quality received from its benefits and the price. It is determined by dividing quality by price measurements. If the quality is perceived to be low as in the first formula below, the perceived value is low. Likewise, if the perceived quality received from a purchase is high relative to its price, the perceived value is high. This is illustrated in the second formula.

$$\frac{\text{Quality (low)}}{\text{Price}} = \textbf{Value (low)}$$

$$\frac{\text{Quality (high)}}{\text{Price}} = \textbf{Value (high)}$$

To increase the perceived value of your product or service, stress its unique features and benefits.

2. Explain the return on investment—Assume a salesperson is selling an expensive photocopy machine. It produces copies 30 percent faster than the competitor's model, but it costs more. The higher price could be justified by calculating the wage savings for the time spent standing at the machine waiting for copies to be run.

3. Calculate the total cost of ownership over the life of the product—The cost of ownership is made up of the initial price plus the other costs related to its use. A furnace for a home that is 95 percent energy efficient might cost $750 more than one that is 70 percent energy efficient, but the cost of natural gas to heat a home would be substantially less with the first furnace. With the more expensive furnace, calculate the savings in the cost of natural gas over the 20-year life of the furnace and compare it with the $750 higher price.

4. Break down the price to smaller units—The cost to a retailer of a half-page newspaper advertisement might be $2,000, but it would cost only four cents per reader. The price of an automobile could be $25,000 but the monthly lease payments are only $295.

Two-Day Sales Training Workshop

Type of Objection	Objection	Strategy to Resolve Objection	Proof and Visual Aids
Need	"My salespeople don't need your workshop because they are already well trained."	Ask the sales manager what formal training each salesperson has had. Find out how current it is. Point out that the workshop involves improving skills that are lacking in his or her salespeople.	Show him or her a list of the topics covered in the workshop. Provide some details of each topic. Quote from two testimonial letters written by experienced salespeople who completed the course.
Product/Service	"We think on-the-job training is more effective."	Compare and contrast the skills that can be developed using on-the-job versus formal training. Point out that a combination of both training methods should be used.	Use the article called "The Advantages and Disadvantages of On-the-Job Sales Training," which appeared in a trade magazine. Provide a diagram of how the two training methods can be integrated.
Source	"I have never heard of your firm."	Provide a brief history of the firm. Discuss the qualifications of its key executives, especially of the person who will conduct the workshop.	Show the prospect a list of some of the firm's clients and an article from the local newspaper that praised the firm. Use a photograph of the firm's top executives and workshop leader.
Price/Money	"Your price of $490 for each participant is too high."	Justify the price based on return on investment.	Share two case histories with the prospect. Point out that these firms experienced a 10 percent increase in sales after completing the workshop.
Time	"Call me back in a week or so."	Use a concession. Point out that if he or she makes a decision right now, you will give each participant a free copy of the book called *Success Stories of the World's Best Salespeople* valued at $29.	Show the prospect a sample of the book. Discuss the Table of Contents with him or her. Mention some of the people who are profiled in the book.

5. Sell the value added—A higher price could be justified by explaining the value your company adds to the purchase, such as fast delivery, free repair or maintenance service, technical assistance, or extensive consumer advertising and promotional support.

6. Show the prospect a lower-priced model in your line.

7. Prove that a higher-priced option will increase the prospect's profits—A product that costs the consumer more might also

provide more margin of profit to the retailer. For example, a DVD player, which costs the consumer $300, might offer the retailer a $120 profit margin, while a $150 model provides only a $60 profit margin.

Whenever you discuss price with the prospect, avoid using such terms as "cheap" or "cheaper." "Cheap" indicates poor quality. Also, replace "cost" with "investment."

How to Resolve Time Objections

Time objections are those related to allowing the salesperson to achieve his or her sales call objective during *this* sales call. They are stalls. The prospect might say, "I want to wait until next week before I decide to buy" or "I have to discuss this matter with my boss." If it is a legitimate time objection, you must provide some compelling reasons to commit today rather than waiting. Refer to the Buy Now Method of Closing the Sale on page 107 for examples of how to resolve this objection. Use one of the five methods presented to resolve your time objection.

Examples of Resolving Objections

In the Handling Objections Planning Guide on pages 98 through 102, you will be asked to identify five objections to your product or service and to provide features, benefits, proof, visual aids, and dramatization that will resolve each one. Examples of how to Handle Objections for a two-day sales training workshop that is being presented to a sales manager are on page 87. Examples of how to Handle Objections for Fusion are provided on pages 92 through 96.

When to Resolve Objections

Prospects may offer objections at any time during the sales presentation. It is generally advisable to try to resolve each objection as it arises. Postponement may alienate the prospect. However, if a prospect offers a price objection early in the presentation before you have had a chance to discuss important features and benefits, it may be advisable to postpone addressing this objection. Assure him or her you will address these concerns after more details about the product or service are given.

Following is a discussion of the steps in Handling Objections.

Steps in Handling Objections

Step 1. Acknowledge the Prospect's Concern

When you **acknowledge objections**, you are implying both interest in the prospect's concerns and appreciation of the fact that he or she voiced them. If the prospect did not voice objections, you could not resolve them. If you do not resolve them, you will not achieve your sales call objective. When you acknowledge the objection, do not imply that you agree with it. Following are some ways to acknowledge objections:

"That's a good point."

"I appreciate your interest."

"I can understand your concern."

"That's a reservation I might have, too."

"It's a good idea to consider that issue."

"You have every right to question that point."

"I understand how you feel."

"I had another customer that had the same concern, at first."

Step 2. Clarify the Objection and Identify the Problem/Need

Clarifying an objection means asking questions pertaining to the objection to ensure you fully understand it. What the prospect says and means are often two different things. When the prospect elaborates on the objection, it helps to defuse it. Clarifying also allows you time to think of what benefits and proof you will use to resolve the objection, while regaining control of the interview. Clarifying does not mean repeating the objection word for word. The questions and comments that follow can be used to begin the clarifying process:

"What is it that you like about _____?"

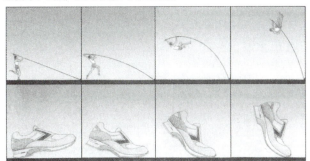

"Could you be more specific?"

"Why do you say that?"

"Would you elaborate on that for me?"

"Please tell me more."

"May I ask why you feel that way?"

Continue asking clarifying questions until the objection has been clearly identified. The following dialogue is an example of how you might converse with your prospect in order to clarify an objection:

PROSPECT:	Your price is too high (*price/money objection*).
SALESPERSON:	That's a good point (*acknowledgment*). What price are you paying now (*clarifier*)?
PROSPECT:	$37.49 per unit, which is $4 less than your price.
SALESPERSON:	To what model of my competitor's are you referring (*clarifier*)?
PROSPECT:	It's their model #2702.
SALESPERSON:	(*The problem has been identified.*) The #2702 is their discount model. It doesn't have some of the features ours does. Let me show you the difference and why ours is worth $4 more.

The following is another example in which clarifying questions revealed the real objection. The salesperson is selling a $10,000 computer system to an office manager.

PROSPECT:	I think I need some more time before I decide (*time objection*).
SALESPERSON:	I can understand how you feel (*acknowledgment*). Is there anything in particular you need to think about (*clarifier*)?
PROSPECT:	No. I just need a little more time.
SALESPERSON:	Do you have concerns about this computer system (*clarifier*)?
PROSPECT:	No. This is the one our company needs.

SALESPERSON:	Could it be the $10,000 investment (*clarifier*)?
PROSPECT:	Well, yes. That's a lot of money. We just can't come up with that much at this time. (*price/money objection; problem identified*).

The objection started out as a time objection, but clarifying questions brought out the real objection; a lack of money, which is a price/money objection. Since the problem has been identified, the salesperson can proceed to Step 3 and address the real objection.

Step 3. Provide Features, Benefits, and Proof to Resolve the Objection—Use Visual Aids and Dramatization

In the Securing Desire section of the presentation, we used features, advantages, benefits, proof, visual aids, and dramatization to convince the prospect that our product or service would solve problems or satisfy needs. Your strategy in Handling Objections is the same. Refer to the discussion on pages 28 through 36 concerning these topics.

Your Features-Benefits Worksheet on pages 43 through 46 should provide the information you need to resolve the objections. You may find, however, that it does not have benefits to resolve all your objections. If this is the case, add features, benefits, proof, and visual aids to the worksheet so all your objections can be resolved.

In the real world, salespeople do not make a sale on every call. Prospects frequently offer objections that cannot be resolved. However, this section is structured to allow salespeople to resolve the objections they get during the Handling Objections role play.

Step 4. Offer a Trial Close

Do not continue with your presentation if the prospect is still voicing an objection. It must be resolved before you can expect to close. A **trial close** is a question that asks the prospect if you have resolved the objection. If you have resolved it, proceed to Step 5. If you have not, go back to Step 2 and start the process over again. A trial close also gives the prospect another opportunity to give you a buying signal. It helps to measure the buying temperature: "cold," "warm," "hot."

The following questions are good trial closes:

"Does that address your concern?"

"Have I resolved that issue?"

"Do you have any more reservations about (objection)?"

"Does that make sense to you?"

"How does that sound?"

"Is this the answer you are seeking?"

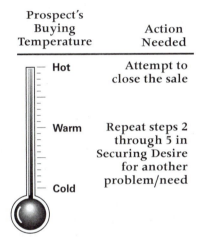

Prospect's Buying Temperature	Action Needed
Hot	Attempt to close the sale
Warm	Repeat steps 2 through 5 in Securing Desire for another problem/need
Cold	

"Do you agree this isn't a problem?"

"Are we together on this?"

Step 5. Close or Go Back to Step 2 in Securing Desire

If the prospect seems ready to close, do so, even if you have more problems your product or service will solve and benefits to support them. If the prospect does not seem ready to close, go back to Step 2 in Securing Desire. Identify another problem/need and support it with features, benefits, proof, and visual aids. Refer to the "Steps in a Sales Presentation" diagram on the inside front cover. The arrows illustrate this process.

Example of Handling Objections

The following is an example of the salesperson-prospect dialogue for the Fusion Handling Objections section. Note there are five objections; one for each of the Five Buying Decisions.

PLANNING GUIDE—FUSION HANDLING OBJECTIONS

Salesperson-Prospect Dialogue

Need Objection

PROSPECT: I don't have room on the shelf for another line of running shoes.

Step 1. Acknowledge concern

SALESPERSON: I've had other dealers mention that, too.

Step 2. Clarify

SALESPERSON: Do you keep a record of sales for each item you stock?

PROSPECT: Yes. We have a computerized inventory control system.

SALESPERSON: Can we take a look at it?

PROSPECT: I'll get it.

Step 3. Features, benefits, proof, visual aids, and dramatization

SALESPERSON: You mentioned earlier that Reebok ERS wasn't selling very well. As you can see here, you have only sold two pairs in the past two months. Penny, you could feature this item at a special price and sell all your stock to make room for Fusion.

Also, you should consider the fact that this is a specialty store that caters to serious runners. Your customers will be seeing our ads in <u>Runner's World</u>, <u>Running Times</u>, and <u>Michigan Runner</u>. They will be coming to your store with the expectation of being able to buy Fusion.

Plus, Fusion is on the cutting edge of technology. As I mentioned before, we have the Propulsion Plate System and HydroFlow pad. (Give her the samples of the Propulsion Plate and HydroFlow pad again.) These features have been tested and proven to improve performance and reduce injuries. Fusion is superior to the Reebok ERS shoe.

Step 4. Trial close

SALESPERSON: Wouldn't you agree?

PLANNING GUIDE—FUSION HANDLING OBJECTIONS (CONTINUED)

Salesperson-Prospect Dialogue

Product/Service Objection

> PROSPECT: The Nike rep was in the other day and showed me the new 180 Air. I like that shoe better.

Step 1. Acknowledge concern

> SALESPERSON: The 180 is a good shoe.

Step 2. Clarify

> SALESPERSON: Penny, what is it that you like about their product?

> PROSPECT: It has extra cushioning.

Step 3. Features, benefits, proof, visual aids, and dramatization

> SALESPERSON: That's true. Nike did make the air bag larger. Also, the term "180" comes from the fact that you can see the air bag 180 degrees around the heel of the shoe. But the shoe does not have any new technology. Nike has had the air bag since 1979 and the fact you can see it doesn't improve a runner's performance.
>
> Fusion has the Propulsion Plate System and the HydroFlow pad to improve performance and reduce injuries. Recently, Fusion won the "Best Running Shoe" award at the Exhibition of Sports and Leisure in London, England. It was rated superior to the 180 in design, aesthetics, and value. (Show article, which details the ratings.) The expert judges felt that Fusion is a superior shoe.

Step 4. Trial close

> SALESPERSON: Have I resolved that issue?

PLANNING GUIDE—FUSION HANDLING OBJECTIONS
(CONTINUED)

Salesperson-Prospect Dialogue

Source Objection

> PROSPECT: Brooks is a small company compared to Nike and Reebok.

Step 1. Acknowledge concern

> SALESPERSON: Size is something to consider.

Step 2. Clarify

> SALESPERSON: Could you be more specific, Penny?

> PROSPECT: They probably spend a lot more money in research and development than Brooks does.

Step 3. Features, benefits, proof, visual aids, and dramatization

> SALESPERSON: You may be right. I don't know how much they spend in R & D. I do know, however, that since 1975, Brooks has led the way in new running shoe technology. (Show "Technical Highlights" page.)
>
> Here is a chronological list of some of our innovations. In 1975, Brooks was the first to introduce the ethylene vinyl acetate (EVA) midsole for improved cushioning. The Diagonal Rollbar was introduced in 1982. It reduces excessive side-to-side motion, which reduces injuries. In 1991, it was the Kinetic Wedge. This feature allows the foot to move in a natural motion, which reduces fatigue. HydroFlow came along in 2003. And now it's the Propulsion Plate System.
>
> These innovations were developed by an expert team of world-class runners, scientists, and engineers, along with the Biomechanics Evaluation Lab at Michigan State University. So you can be assured that when you buy a Brooks shoe, you are getting the best that technology has to offer.

Step 4. Trial close

> SALESPERSON: Do you agree this isn't a problem?

PLANNING GUIDE—FUSION HANDLING OBJECTIONS (CONTINUED)

Salesperson-Prospect Dialogue

Price-Money Objection

PROSPECT: What is your price?

SALESPERSON: Our suggested retail price is $124.95.

PROSPECT: My customers won't pay that much for a shoe.

Step 1. Acknowledge concern

SALESPERSON: I'm glad you raised that issue, Penny.

Step 2. Clarify

SALESPERSON: Do you stock any shoes that are priced over $100?

PROSPECT: The Nike Air Max is priced at $110.

SALESPERSON: What kind of turnover does it have?

PROSPECT: Pretty good but not the best.

Step 3. Features, benefits, proof, visual aids, and dramatization

SALESPERSON: It's incredible what people will pay for state-of-the-art athletic products these days. A good tennis racquet costs over $500, and it's hard to find a nice set of golf clubs for under $1,000. As I mentioned before, Penny, Fusion is designed for the serious runners who shop in your store. They want the latest technology and will pay for it, provided it is a good value.

    I have a list here that shows how good a value Fusion is. (Show "Value" visual aid.) First, I have mentioned that Fusion will dramatically improve running performance due to the Propulsion Plate System. Second, the HydroFlow pad provides cushioning, which will reduce foot, ankle, and knee injuries. Third, we have an anatomically correct fit, which improves comfort and an extremely durable outsole so it lasts longer. And finally, Fusion offers contemporary styling. These features make Fusion an outstanding value, which will result in high sales and profits for this store.

Step 4. Trial close

SALESPERSON: Considering these factors, would you agree Fusion is a good value?

PLANNING GUIDE—FUSION HANDLING OBJECTIONS
(CONTINUED)

Salesperson-Prospect Dialogue

Time Objection

    PROSPECT: It's only February. Why don't you come back after the weather breaks?

Step 1. Acknowledge concern

    SALESPERSON: I understand how you feel.

Step 2. Clarify

    SALESPERSON: When do sales of your running shoes begin to pick up?

    PROSPECT: Around the first of April.

Step 3. Features, benefits, proof, visual aids, and dramatization

    SALESPERSON: That's when most of my retailers experience a big surge in sales. I mentioned earlier that our advertising for Fusion begins with the April issues of <u>Runner's World</u>, <u>Running Times</u>, and <u>Michigan Runner</u>. These publications hit the newsstands on March 15th. If you wait until April to place your order, you will miss out on the sales our initial ads will generate. And you will have a lot of disappointed customers.

Step 4. Trial close

    SALESPERSON: You don't want to disappoint your customers and pass up those sales and profits, do you, Penny?

Preparing to Role Play

Planning Guide Form—Handling Objections

This chapter explained the content of the Handling Objections section of the presentation. Complete the following steps to prepare to role play Handling Objections.

1. Refer to your completed Features-Benefits Worksheet on pages 43 through 46. It should contain most of the features, benefits, proof, visual aids, and dramatization needed to overcome objections. If you lack some benefits, add them to the worksheet. Also review the rating form on page 104 to ensure you understand how the role play of Handling Objections will be evaluated.

2. Detach the perforated form from the text that is needed to role play Handling Objections (pages 98 through 102). Your prospect will need it during the role play.

3. Use a number 2 pencil to complete the form so that changes can be made later. Number 2 pencils are recommended because hard-lead pencils do not produce good photocopies. Print neatly so that your prospect will understand what is written.

4. Complete the Planning Guide form for Handling Objections. Refer to the example for Fusion on pages 92 through 96. Make sure you have five objections, one for each of the Five Buying Decisions, and are written as statements not questions. Provide a complete dialogue of what you and the prospect say. Use several visual aids to communicate features, benefits, and proof.

5. Make a photocopy of the completed Planning Guide form.

6. Practice the Handling Objections role play by reading the salesperson-prospect dialogue several times out loud.

How the Role Play Will Be Conducted

Your instructor may have you role play Handling Objections. If not, you should role play it on your own or with another person. Familiarize yourself with the instructions beginning on page 59. You will not be role playing the Approach or Securing Desire, only Handling Objections. Begin seated at the prospect's desk.

The prospect will allow you to resolve each objection with one counter-benefit. (In the real world, it may take several counters to resolve an objection, and you may not be able to resolve some objections.) You should respond to each objection using the four steps you have learned. Do not try to close the sale. Stop at the last trial close.

Materials Needed to Role Play Handling Objections

You will need your Setting the Scene form on page 60, five-page Planning Guide, a photocopy of the Planning Guide for the prospect, Handling Objections rating form, product samples, visual aids, and text to successfully role play Handling Objections. If you do not have access to a photocopy machine to reproduce your Planning Guide for the prospect, make a typed or handwritten copy of the salesperson-prospect dialogue. Include the titles of the steps.

PLANNING GUIDE—HANDLING OBJECTIONS

Salesperson-Prospect Dialogue

Refer to the example of the completed Planning Guide on pages 92 through 96.

Need Objection *(Detach this perforated form. The prospect will need it during the role play. Fill this form out neatly in number 2 pencil. Write the prospect's objection here as a declarative statement, not a question. Use the prospect's name throughout.)*

Step 1. Acknowledge concern *(See page 88.)*

Step 2. Clarify *(See pages 88 and 90.)*

Step 3. Features, benefits, proof, visual aids, and dramatization *(Refer to your Features-Benefits Worksheet on pages 43 through 46. Also see pages 85 and 86 for ideas to resolve need objections.)*

Step 4. Trial close *(See pages 90 and 91.)*

PLANNING GUIDE—HANDLING OBJECTIONS
(continued)

Salesperson-Prospect Dialogue

Product/Service Objection *(Write the prospect's objection here.)*

Step 1. Acknowledge concern *(Use a different acknowledgment statement than the first one.)*

Step 2. Clarify *(Use a different clarifying question than the first one.)*

Step 3. Features, benefits, proof, visual aids, and dramatization *(Refer to pages 85 and 86 for ideas to resolve product/service objections.)*

Step 4. Trial close *(Use a different trial close than the first one.)*

PLANNING GUIDE—HANDLING OBJECTIONS
(continued)

Salesperson-Prospect Dialogue

Source Objection *(This is an objection related to doing business with you or your company.)*

Step 1. Acknowledge concern

Step 2. Clarify

Step 3. Features, benefits, proof, visual aids, and dramatization *(Refer to pages 85 and 86 for ideas to resolve source objections.)*

Step 4. Trial close

PLANNING GUIDE—HANDLING OBJECTIONS
(continued)

Salesperson-Prospect Dialogue

Price-Money Objection *(PROSPECT: Be sure you know what the price is before you offer this objection.)*

Step 1. Acknowledge concern

Step 2. Clarify

Step 3. Features, benefits, proof, visual aids, and dramatization *(Refer to pages 86 through 88 for ideas to resolve price objections.)*

Step 4. Trial close

PLANNING GUIDE—HANDLING OBJECTIONS
(continued)

Salesperson-Prospect Dialogue

Time Objection *(This is an objection related to allowing you to achieve your call objective during this sales call. The prospect is trying to stall.)*

Step 1. Acknowledge concern

Step 2. Clarify

Step 3. Features, benefits, proof, visual aids, and dramatization *(Use one of the "Buy Now Methods" of closing the sale on page 107 to resolve this objection. Provide a compelling reason why the prospect should give you a commitment during this sales call.)*

Step 4. Trial close

Concepts To Know

Handling objections

Five buying decisions

Need objections

Product/service objections

Source objections

Price/money objections

Time objections

Acknowledging an objection

Clarifying an objection

Trial close

Assignments

1. A Web site that offers consulting and training for salespeople is http://www.thesalescoach.com. Visit the site and review the services offered. Find an article related to this course by selecting "Enter" at the bottom of the home page, then select "Free Library." Develop a report on the site and what you learned from the article. If you do not find a relevant article, go to a college or public library and search databases with full-text articles on selling. ABI/Inform is an example. The librarian may have to give you a password to access the databases.

2. Complete the Handling Objections section of your presentation by following the directions on page 97. Detach the perforated form on pages 98 through 102. Fill it out using a number 2 pencil so changes can be made later. Use the completed form for Fusion on pages 92 through 96 as a guide. The Features-Benefits Worksheet completed in Chapter 5 contains much of the information needed. Prepare typed visual aids that are needed to communicate features, benefits, and proof.

3. Prepare to role play Handling Objections. Follow the instructions on page 97.

Handling Objections Rating Form (25 Points)

Salesperson's Company: _____   Hour: _____

Product/Service: _____   Salesperson's Name: _____

Prospect's Company: _____

Objections Assigned to Role Play: <u>Need, product/service, source, price, and/or time objections.</u>

	Possible Score	Actual Score		
		Record Scores of Three Role Plays		
–Ability in acknowledging the prospect's concern after each objection	2	_____	_____	_____
–Ability in clarifying each objection	4	_____	_____	_____
–Ability in providing features and benefits relevant to each objection	7	_____	_____	_____
–Ability in offering proof, when appropriate	4	_____	_____	_____
–Ability in offering a trial close after each objection	2	_____	_____	_____
–Ability in using visual aids where appropriate	3	_____	_____	_____
–Ability in being enthusiastic, smiling, and using the prospect's name	3	_____	_____	_____
Total	25 pts.	_____	_____	_____

Coach's notes and comments: _____

Chapter 9

Closing the Sale and Building Customer Relations

Objective of Closing the Sale

The ultimate goal of any sales presentation is **Closing the Sale**. At this point in the presentation, you get a commitment from the prospect for an order or a plan of action. Closing is achieving your sales call objective.

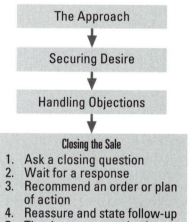

Closing the Sale
1. Ask a closing question
2. Wait for a response
3. Recommend an order or plan of action
4. Reassure and state follow-up
5. Thank prospect and exit

Preparing to Close the Sale

When to Close

Inexperienced salespeople often wonder when it is appropriate to try to Close the Sale. You should close when the prospect indicates he or she is ready to close, in other words, when the buying temperature is "hot." This can be at the beginning, middle, or end of the presentation. Often it is after you have asked a trial close question. Whenever the prospect gives you a buying signal, try to Close the Sale.

A **buying signal** is anything a person does or says that suggests he or she is ready to offer a commitment. You must listen to and observe the prospect to identify signals. The following is a list of common buying signals.

Looking Ahead

After studying this chapter and completing the assignments, you should be able to:

1. recognize buying signals offered by prospects,

2. ask for a commitment from prospects using several closing methods,

3. develop and effectively role play the Closing the Sale section of the sales presentation, and

4. build customer relations through follow-up after the sales call.

1. After successfully handling a major objection

   SALESPERSON: "Have I resolved the issue of price for you?"

   PROSPECT: "I can see it's worth the price."

2. When the prospect gives enthusiastic agreement to a benefit

   "Our company could really use something like that."

   "That's a real advantage."

   "That's exactly what we've been looking for."

   "When we place our first order . . ."

   "That would solve a problem we've been having."

   "I'm interested."

   "That really makes sense."

   "I never thought of that before."

   "I guess we could give it a try."

3. When the prospect asks questions that suggest he or she is ready to offer a commitment

   "When can you deliver?"

   "What sizes does it come in?"

   "Do you offer any discounts?"

   "Is that item in stock?"

   "Do you charge for installation?"

4. When the prospect provides nonverbal signs that suggest he or she is ready to commit

   Suddenly relaxes body.

   Nods head in approval.

   Smiles in agreement.

   Picks up the product and examines it closely.

   Begins to read the sales agreement.

5. At the end of the presentation after all problems and needs in Securing Desire have been addressed.

You may get several buying signals throughout the presentation. Each time you do, try to close. If the prospect is not ready to be closed, he or she will ask for more information or offer an objection. Provide the information or resolve the objection, then try to close again if you get a buying signal.

Closing Methods

There are a number of different methods to Close the Sale. It is important to know how to use several, because no single method is appropriate under all circumstances. Below are five of the most common methods.

Direct Method—Ask for a commitment directly. This involves stating your sales call objective that was identified in Chapter 4 as a question.

> "Do I have your commitment to buy this word processor?"

> "May we schedule a tour of our hotel and meeting rooms?"

> "Can I count on you to begin using our agency to book all of your executive travel beginning the first of the month?"

Minor Point Method—Rather than asking the prospect *if* he or she wants to offer a commitment, ask *what, when,* or *how* he or she wants to commit.

> "How about installation next week?"

> "Would delivery the first of the month be soon enough?"

> "Should this purchase be billed to the home office?"

> "Should the order be marked RUSH?"

Alternative Choice Method—Ask the prospect which of two variations is desired. The choices could be between such things as two models, colors, delivery dates, installation dates, payment plans, or quantities to buy.

"May we begin offering our service this week or is next week best for you?"

"Would this model or our deluxe model best suit your needs?"

"Shall we write the order for 1,000 units or would 750 be enough?"

"Would you rather lease or buy the equipment?"

Buy Now Method—Provide some compelling reason why the prospect should commit today rather than waiting, then ask for a commitment. End each method below with a question that asks for a commitment.

Trial offer: "I can see that you have some reservations to buying our FAX machine today. Why don't I bring one over and let you try it out for a week free of charge. Okay?"

Standing Room Only: "Our hotel meeting rooms get booked up really fast. If you don't reserve the rooms for your meeting today, they may not be available. Do I have your commitment?"

Impending event: "Our price is going up $215 in four weeks. If you buy now, I can guarantee you this price. Shall we write up the order?"

Concession: "Normally we don't do this, but if I can get a commitment now, I'll give you a one-year service contract at half price. Okay?"

Ideal time to buy: "As soon as the weather breaks, a lot more people will be playing tennis. If you buy now, the tennis rackets will be in your store and you can begin to realize all the profits we talked about. What do you say?"

Summary Method—Briefly summarize three or four major benefits you mentioned in the presentation, then ask for a commitment. Your last benefit should be the general benefit used in the Approach. End this method with a question that asks for a commitment.

"Let me summarize the major benefits we've talked about this morning, Mr. Jones. First, our sales training workshop is a comprehensive program that will improve the skills of both your new and experienced salespeople. Second, they will learn how to conduct better sales presentations and manage their time more productively. And finally, your company will experience an increase in sales and profits. Shall we schedule the workshop?"

Notice that all closing methods end with a question. You must ask for a commitment to close the sale.

Attitude Toward Closing

To be successful in Closing the Sale, you must have the proper closing attitude. First, expect that you will close during your sales call. Assume the prospect wants to be on the winning team. If you do not possess this positive attitude and this confidence in your company and product or service, the prospect will sense it and be less likely to offer a commitment. Second, provide only the features, benefits, proof, and visual aids necessary to close. Your mission is not to overwhelm the prospect with your knowledge of your industry, company, and product or service. Finally, do not be afraid to ask for a commitment. The prospect will respond to your closing question by either agreeing to commit, by offering an objection, or by identifying more problems or needs that need to be addressed with features and benefits. Regardless of the response, you will know what to do. If the prospect's response is favorable, continue the closing sequence. If an objection is offered, handle it using the steps discussed in Chapter 8, then try to close again if you get a buying signal. If the prospect feels he or she must be shown how the product or service can solve more problems or satisfy more needs, return to Securing Desire. Remember prospects expect to be asked for a commitment. They want you to help them make the decision. So ask a closing question and Close the Sale.

Building Customer Relations through Follow-up

Most of this text has focused on developing and conducting an effective sales presentation. In the short term, good presentations will have a substantial impact on sales. However, in the long term, establishing positive relationships with customers by following up after the initial presentation will result in even greater sales. Assume, for example, that you are a salesperson for Brooks Shoe, Inc., calling on a retail store manager. The initial order for the Fusion running shoe might be $1,500. If you go out of your way to make sure the retailer is happy with the initial purchase, it will increase the retailer's confidence in you and your company. Provided the product generates sufficient turnover, the loyalty and goodwill created could result in future sales of tens of thousands of dollars. **Follow-up** activities, such as those listed next, will enable you to build customer relations and long-term sales volume.

After the initial presentation, contact the customer in person, by letter, or by email or telephone to:

1. ensure satisfaction after delivery of your product or use of your service. Make sure the customer's needs were satisfied;

2. report the status of open orders, including production schedules, the availability of products or services, or delivery dates to keep the customer informed of progress;

3. initiate installation, maintenance, or repairs of the product;

4. schedule engineers or technicians to meet with the customer;

5. train customer personnel on how to operate the product (e.g., a photocopy machine);

6. train wholesale or retail customer salespeople on how to sell the product;

7. send or deliver additional brochures, literature, proposals, or contracts;

8. help build a display or merchandise the product in retail stores after receiving the shipment;

9. answer customer questions related to the purchase;

10. handle customer complaints, such as late delivery, product quality problems, out-of-stock conditions, billing errors, or damaged products due to shipping;

11. schedule a meeting to make another sales presentation with the goal of discovering new needs and getting additional orders;

12. get referrals for new prospects from customers.

Some salespeople go beyond the activities mentioned here and send "thank you" letters to customers, birthday and holiday cards, and personal notes of congratulations when customers earn promotions. In summary, most successful salespeople have a long-term perspective on solving customer problems and satisfying their needs while building relationships through extensive follow-up activities and providing good customer service.

Following are the steps in Closing the Sale.

Steps in Closing the Sale

Step 1. Ask a Closing Question

When you get a buying signal, often after a trial close, ask for a commitment using an appropriate closing method. The Direct Method can be used any time. The Minor Point Method is excellent when the prospect seems afraid to make a decision. If the prospect seems interested and has narrowed his or her choices somewhat, try the Alternative Choice Method. The Buy Now Method is appropriate when you get a time objection. At the end of the presentation, when all the problem and needs in Securing Desire have been addressed, the Summary Method is a good choice. Since you may have several opportunities to Close the Sale, use the method that is appropriate for the existing circumstances.

Step 2. Wait For a Response

When you have asked a closing question, there may be a period of silence. Don't be afraid of the silence. The prospect is considering the Five Buying Decisions: "Do I *need* this type of product or service?" "Will this specific brand of *product or service* satisfy my needs?" "Is this the *source* from whom I should buy?" "Is the *price* right?" and "Is the *time* to buy now?" Let the prospect be the first one to speak after you have asked a closing question. If you talk first, you may lose this chance to close. If the prospect is not ready to be closed, he or she will either ask for more information or offer an objection. If so, provide the information or handle the objection, then try to close again if you get a buying signal.

Step 3. Recommend an Order or Plan of Action and Confirm the Details

If your sales call objective is to write an order or get a contract signed, have one to fill out during your presentation. If you do not have an order form, make one up like the one for Fusion on page 110. Recommend a specific quantity, considering what is realistic for the prospect to buy. Confirm the delivery date and billing and shipping addresses. If the prospect is going to resell the product, be sure to stress the profit per unit and total profit for the quantity you are recommending. The profit benefit helps justify the investment being made. The following is how the dialogue might sound if you were selling Fusion to a retail store manager.

SALESPERSON: Shall we write up the order for 18 pairs of the men's sizes (*Direct Close*)?

PROSPECT: Yes, I guess so.

SALESPERSON: (*Pulls out the order form and begins filling it out. The sample order form is on page 110.*) Okay, that's 18 pairs of our item number 4870, Fusion shoes.

The unit price is $67 per pair. That comes to a total investment of $1,206. Now since you'll have 46 percent markup on this item, you'll enjoy profits of $57.95 per pair and total profits of $1,043.10 for this order.

When do you want delivery?

PROSPECT: The first of the month would be soon enough.

SALESPERSON: (*Writes the date on the order form.*) Is this the correct address for shipping and billing?

PROSPECT: Yes it is.

SALESPERSON: If you would just authorize the paperwork, we can start processing the order right away. (*Salesperson gives the order form and a pen for the prospect's signature.*)

Your sales call objective might be such that it is not appropriate to write an order. For example, if you were selling the use of meeting rooms for a hotel to a sales manager, your sales call objective might be to convince him or her to accompany you to the hotel to see your facilities. Rather than writing an order, you are requesting a plan of action. You would be combining Steps 1, 2, and 3 above. Here's how the dialogue might go:

SALESPERSON: Let me make a suggestion. Why don't we set up a time that would be convenient for you to come down to our hotel and see our facilities (*plan of action*)? Would this week or next week be best for you (*Alternative Choice Method*)?

PROSPECT: (*Looks at calendar.*) This week is bad. Next Tuesday looks good.

SALESPERSON: That's perfect. How about 11:30? That way we can have lunch so you can see how good our food is in our hotel restaurant.

PROSPECT: Fine.

SALESPERSON: Why don't I pick you up here at 11:30 next Tuesday (*confirm the details*)?

PROSPECT: Okay.

Step 4. Reassure the Prospect and State Your Follow-up Plan

People often have misgivings about something they buy. They wonder if they have made the right decision. They feel better about the decision if they are reassured. Give prospects a verbal pat on the back. Tell them that they have made the right decision to accept your proposal.

ORDER FORM

BROOKS SHOE, INC.
9341 Courtland Dr.
Rockford, MI 49351
616-866-5500

BILL TO: Taylor Sports, Inc.
2122 Main Street
Grand Rapids, MI
49507

DATE OF ORDER: February 4, 20—

SHIP ON: March 1, 20—

SALESPERSON: J. Dykehouse

Quantity	Item Number	Description	Unit Price	Total Amount
18 pairs	4870	Fusion Shoes — Men's Sizes 7, 7½, 8, 11½, 12, 13 one pair of each. Balance of sizes two pairs each.	$67.00 per pair	$1,206.00
		Total Amount of Order		$1,206.00

SHIP TO:

Same as above.

Penny Taylor
Buyer's Name—Print

Penny Taylor
Buyer's Signature

Prospects also want to know that you are going to make sure the order or plan of action they have agreed to will be taken care of properly. By stating your follow-up plan, you are confirming to them that you appreciate their trust and will not consider your job complete until they reap the benefits of the purchase. Refer to the follow-up activities discussed on pages 107 and 108. Use one that is appropriate for your product or service. This portion of Closing the Sale for Fusion might sound like the following:

SALESPERSON: You have definitely made the right decision to buy Fusion, Penny. It is going to be the big winner in the running shoe category this season (*reassure*).

What I'll do is input your order tonight and make a point to come back just after you receive your shipment, so I can put up some of our point-of-sale material. I'll also have brochures that will explain the benefits of Fusion to your salespeople and customers (*follow-up*).

The sales representative for the hotel might say:

SALESPERSON: Your time will be well spent when you come down and see our facility. It's perfect for your needs (*reassure*).

When I get back to the office, I'll check and make sure the date you want is open. Would it be all right if I call you this afternoon to confirm it (*follow-up*)?

Begin to pack up your visual aids and other materials in preparation for your exit.

PLANNING GUIDE—FUSION CLOSING THE SALE

Salesperson-Prospect Dialogue

Step 1. Ask a closing question.

Direct Method

SALESPERSON: Shall we write up an order for Fusion?

Minor Point Method

SALESPERSON: Would delivery on March 1st be soon enough?

Alternative Choice Method

SALESPERSON: Our women's line will be out in mid-April, Penny. Do you want to order the men's and women's lines today or do you want to wait until next month to place your order for the women's line?

PROSPECT: Let's go ahead with just the men's line for now.

Buy Now Method

SALESPERSON: (Standing Room Only) The demand for this shoe is going to be very high this spring. If you place your order today, Penny, I can guarantee we will have adequate inventory to meet your needs. Do I have your commitment?

Summary Method

SALESPERSON: Let me summarize the major benefits we've talked about this morning, Penny. First, the HydroFlow pad and Propulsion Plate System will improve running performance and reduce injuries. Second, our advertising and promotional program will create awareness for Fusion resulting in high sales in your store. And, finally, Fusion will increase the profits of your athletic shoe department. Shall we go ahead with it?

PLANNING GUIDE—FUSION CLOSING THE SALE
(continued)

Salesperson-Prospect Dialogue

Step 2. Wait for a response.

Step 3. Recommend an order and confirm the details.

SALESPERSON: (Get order form and fill it out.) I recommend that your initial order be 18 pairs; one pair for sizes 7, 7 1/2, 8, 11 1/2 , 12, and 13. We should double up on the more popular sizes. Okay?

PROSPECT: What's my total cost?

SALESPERSON: Let's see. The investment is $67 per pair times 18 pairs. $1,206. And the profit per unit at our suggested retail price of $124.95 is $57.95. So your total profit for this order is $1,043.10. Not bad! Wouldn't you agree?

PROSPECT: Let's go ahead with it.

SALESPERSON: Would delivery the first of the month be soon enough?

PROSPECT: Yes.

SALESPERSON: Is this the correct address for shipping and billing?

PROSPECT: Yes it is.

SALESPERSON: If you would just authorize the paperwork, we can start processing the order right away. (Give order form and pen to the prospect.)

Step 4. Reassure the prospect and state your follow-up plan.

SALESPERSON: You have definitely made the right decision to buy Fusion, Penny. It is going to be the big winner in the running shoe category this season.

What I'll do is input your order tonight and make a point to come back just after you receive your shipment, so I can put up some of our point-of-sale material. I'll also have some information that will explain the benefits of Fusion to your salespeople and customers.

Step 5. Thank the prospect and exit.

SALESPERSON: Thanks very much, Penny. I'll see you in about four weeks.

Step 5. Thank the Prospect and Exit

Since the prospect has just agreed to do what you want, you should show your appreciation by thanking him or her. Do not spend time bringing up more benefits or idle small talk. It might give the prospect time to come up with an objection you cannot resolve. You have achieved your sales call objective, so pack up your materials and exit. Be sure to smile and shake hands on the way out.

Example of Closing the Sale

An example of Closing the Sale for Fusion is on pages 111 and 112. Note that there are closing questions for each of the five methods discussed in this chapter. Steps 3, 4, and 5 are the same regardless of the closing method used.

Preparing to Role Play

Planning Guide Form—Closing the Sale

You can now apply the principles you have learned about Closing the Sale to your own presentation. Complete the following steps to prepare to role play.

1. Detach the perforated form from the text that is needed to role play Closing the Sale (pages 114 and 115). Your prospect will need it when you role play.

2. Use a number 2 pencil to complete the form so that changes can be made later. Print neatly so that your prospect will understand what is written.

3. Review the rating form on page 117 to ensure you understand how the role play of Closing the Sale will be evaluated.

4. Complete the Planning Guide form for Closing the Sale including a closing question for each of the five methods. Refer to the example for Fusion on pages 111 and 112. If you are writing an order or getting a signature on a contract, make up a form like the one on page 110, unless you secured one from your company. Make a photocopy of the completed Planning Guide form.

5. Practice Closing the Sale by reading the salesperson/prospect dialogue several times out loud.

How the Role Play Will Be Conducted

Your instructor may have you role play closing the sale. If not, do so on your own to ensure you are prepared to role play the final presentation. You will role play only the close, so you will begin seated at the prospect's desk. The prospect should not give the salesperson any objections but should allow the salesperson to Close the Sale each time he or she is asked a closing question.

You will role play three closes using three of the five closing methods. One is not contingent on the other. Go through Step 3 (recommend an order or plan of action), Step 4 (reassure the prospect), and Step 5 (thank the prospect and exit) *only on the first closing method you are using*. After you have role played a complete close, sit down again and role play two more closing methods. Following is a list of what should be done by the salesperson, prospect, and coach:

1. Coach assigns three closing methods to the salesperson.

2. Salesperson gives the prospect the photocopy of the Planning Guide form and "sets the scene" by conveying the information on page 60.

3. Salesperson states which closing method will be used first.

4. Salesperson asks a closing question using the closing method and does a complete close, including recommending an order or a plan of action, reassuring and stating his or her follow-up, and thanking the prospect and exiting. The coach fills out the rating form. This closing sequence is completed.

5. Salesperson sits down and states what closing method will be used next. The salesperson asks a closing question using the closing method but does not go through Steps 3, 4, or 5, only Steps 1 and 2.

6. Repeat point 5 above for the third closing method. The role play is now completed.

PLANNING GUIDE—CLOSING THE SALE

Salesperson-Prospect Dialogue

Refer to the example of the completed Planning Guide on pages 111 and 112.

PROSPECT: If you a purchasing something, be sure you know what the price is before you allow the salesperson to Close the Sale.

Step 1. Ask a closing question. *(Detach this perforated form. Your prospect will need it during the role play. Fill out this form neatly in number 2 pencil. Write small. Provide a closing question for each of the five methods below.)*

DIRECT METHOD *(Write your closing question here. See pages 106 and 107.)*

MINOR POINT METHOD

ALTERNATIVE CHOICE METHOD

BUY NOW METHOD *(Use one of the Buy Now Methods of closing on page 107.)*

SUMMARY METHOD

PLANNING GUIDE—CLOSING THE SALE
(continued)

Salesperson-Prospect Dialogue

Step 2. Wait for a response.

Step 3. Recommend an order and confirm the details. *(Steps 3, 4, and 5 are the same regardless of the closing method used on the previous page. See page 109.)*

Step 4. Reassure the prospect and state your follow-up plan. *(See pages 109 and 110.)*

Step 5. Thank the prospect and exit. *(See page 113.)*

Materials Needed to Role Play Closing the Sale

You will need your Setting the Scene form on page 60, two-page completed Planning Guide, a photocopy of the Planning Guide for the prospect, the Closing the Sale rating form, and text to successfully role play Closing the Sale. If you are writing an order or getting a signature on a contract during the close, have a form to complete in the presence of the prospect. An example of an order form is on page 110. Also bring a pen so the prospect can sign the order form. The prospect can ad lib all responses during the close, so if you do not have access to a photocopy machine to reproduce your Planning Guide for your prospect, the role play can be conducted without it.

Concepts To Know

Closing the sale

Buying signal

Closing methods:

Direct

Minor point

Alternative choice

Buy now

Trial offer

Standing room only

Impending event

Concession

Ideal time to buy

Summary

Follow-up

Assignments

1. A Web site that offers training programs for salespeople is http://www.salesxcellence.co.uk. (Note the spelling of "xcellence.") Visit the site and review the services offered. Find an article related to this course by selecting "Resources" located at the bottom of the home page. Develop a report on the site and what you learned from the article. If you do not find a relevant article, go to a college or public library and search databases with full-text articles on selling. ABI/Inform is an example. The librarian may have to give you a password to access the databases.

2. Compete the Closing the Sale section of your presentation by following the directions on page 113 and 116. Detach the perforated form on pages 114 and 115. Your prospect will need it during the role play. Fill it out using a number 2 pencil so changes can be made later. Use the completed form for Fusion on pages 111 and 112 as a guide. Prepare an order form or contract like the one on page 110, if your presentation calls for it.

3. Prepare to role play Closing the Sale. Follow the instructions on pages 113 and 116.

Closing the Sale Rating Form (25 Points)

Salesperson's Company: _____   Hour: _____

Product/Service: _____   Salesperson's Name: _____

Prospect's Company: _____

Closing Methods to Role Play: <u>Direct, minor point, alternative choice, buy now, and/or summary methods.</u>

	Possible Score	Actual Score		
		Record Scores of Three Role Plays		
–Ability in using the assigned Closing Method(s) properly	7	_____	_____	_____
–Ability in waiting for a response, recommending an order or plan of action, and confirming the details. (If an order or contract is required, did the salesperson have a form and secure a signature? If the product is going to be resold by the prospect, were profits per unit and total profits mentioned?)	7	_____	_____	_____
–Ability in reassuring the prospect	3	_____	_____	_____
–Ability in stating a follow-up plan	3	_____	_____	_____
–Ability in thanking the prospect and exiting properly	2	_____	_____	_____
–Ability in being enthusiastic, smiling, and using the prospect's name	3	_____	_____	_____
Total	25 pts.	_____	_____	_____

Coach's notes and comments:

Chapter 10

Role Playing and Writing the Complete Sales Presentation

Other Characteristics of an Effective Sales Presentation

While this text has provided most of what you need to know to conduct an effective presentation, the following are some additional suggestions.

1. Focus your attention on the prospect, not on your product or service.

2. Establish a dialogue (two-way communication), not a monologue, to maintain the prospect's interest and attention.

3. Maintain control, but do not show it. High-pressure salespeople can intimidate prospects. Ask questions, offer choices, and request assistance.

4. Put visual aids directly in front of the prospect.

5. If you do a demonstration, get the prospect physically involved in it.

6. Use proper body language. Maintain eye contact and smile.

7. Avoid objectionable mannerisms, such as chewing gum, tapping your feet, and repeating yourself with "and-ah," "umh," etc.

8. Use the proper speed of delivery—not too fast or too slow.

9. Keep your presentation brief and to the point. Do not be wordy.

10. Maintain a positive, enthusiastic attitude.

11. Project poise and confidence.

Looking Ahead

After studying this chapter and completing the assignments, you should be able to:

1. role play a complete and professional sales presentation as a salesperson and prospect, and

2. prepare a written report that explains the nature and content of the sales presentation including visual aids that are used.

12. Adapt your presentation to the personality style of the prospect.

Personality Styles of Prospects

Every prospect has a different personality. A salesperson must adapt his or her selling style and presentation to the prospect's personality if the sales presentation is to be successful. This adaptation can be particularly difficult on the first meeting with a prospect. The way the prospect responded to an email or acted on the telephone when you called to set up an appointment may give you a clue as to his or her personality, but you can never be sure until you meet face-to-face. The following are suggestions for adapting your presentation, given the personality of the prospect.

Social Personality

The prospect is warm, friendly, and indecisive and has a tendency to talk incessantly and get off the subject. Use an aggressive, hard-sell approach and appeal to emotions. If the prospect spends too much time on small talk, use questions to direct the conversation back to the presentation.

Analytical Personality

The prospect is shy, logical, and objective and asks many questions about the technical details of the product or service. Use facts, figures, and other information (e.g., durability, quality, and dependability) to appeal to the prospect's rational nature. A low-pressure selling style will be the most effective.

Dominant Personality

The prospect is cold, aggressive, and opinionated and may try to rush the salesperson and attempt to take control of the presentation. Use a concise presentation. Make your points and move on. Try to maintain control of the presentation without showing it by asking questions to keep the prospect involved.

Preparing to Role Play the Complete Presentation

Now that you are familiar with the four major sections of a sales presentation, you are ready to put them together and role play a complete presentation. You will be expected to apply everything you have learned in this text. If you have role played each of the four sections of the presentation, you are well prepared to role play the complete presentation. If you have not, begin your preparation by reviewing each of the four parts of a presentation and then role play them.

A successful preparation process involves the following steps:

1. Review your Planning Guide for one part of the presentation.

2. While alone, role play the salesperson-prospect dialogue *out loud*. You must get used to hearing yourself say the words.

3. Evaluate yourself using the appropriate rating form at the end of the chapter for the section you are role playing.

4. Repeat 2 and 3 above until you feel comfortable with a section of the presentation.

5. Role play the section with someone acting as a prospect.

6. Repeat 5 until you are doing everything properly.

7. Role play the complete presentation several times with someone. Tape it and evaluate yourself using the Final Sales Presentation Rating Form on pages 125 and 126.

This process will take several hours over a three- or four-day period to be properly prepared. On the day you are scheduled to give your presentation, spend approximately one hour listening to the tape of your role plays and roughly two hours rehearsing your presentation *out loud*.

Anyone involved in role playing or making an actual sales call gets nervous—even experienced sales representatives. Reread the section in Chapter 1 on "Overcoming Fear" on page 2.

Guidelines for Being a Salesperson

Your instructor may assign another student to be your prospect. If so, the prospect will need the *original copies* of your Planning Guide forms a couple of days before you are scheduled to role play. You must keep two photocopies of these forms. If the nature of your product or service specifically requires a male or a female prospect, let your instructor know ahead of time.

Your instructor may require that you dress in the type of attire a sales representative selling your product or service would wear. In most cases, this means a suit or sport coat and tie for men and a skirt, dress, or suit for women. Sales representatives in some industries do not wear formal dress. For example, someone selling roofing and siding, burglar alarm systems, or vacuum cleaners to homeowners might wear business-casual clothes. Find out the typical attire for a sales representative with your company and dress accordingly.·

When you are role playing Securing Desire, you may have to support only one or two problems/needs. You should attempt to Close the Sale each time you are given a buying signal, even if you there are more problems/needs that could be addressed. You will not lose points for closing early, but you will lose points if you fail to attempt to close when you are given a buying signal.

Your prospect will also lose points if he or she allows you to close before you have been given at least three objections. If the prospect allows you to close early, do so. If your instructor feels you have not had an opportunity to demonstrate your ability to Secure Desire or Handle Objections, he or she will allow you to role play the portions that you did not do the first time. You will not have to repeat anything; you will just role play what was left out.

The prospect may present you with a time objection that involves getting approval from another decision maker. Acknowledge and clarify the objection and try to convince him or her to give you a commitment without the other person's approval. Use the Buy Now Method of closing to resolve the objection.

The guidelines in the section "How the Role Play Will Be Conducted" on pages 59 and 63 are still in effect. Since your prospect will already have your Planning Guide forms, you will not have to provide them when you role play. You cannot call "time out," use your Planning Guides, or use any notes other than visual aids when you role play your complete presentation. Be sure to set the scene before the role play begins by discussing the information on page 60.

Guidelines for Being a Prospect

During the role play, you will be evaluated if you are a prospect, so thorough preparation is necessary. Study the Planning Guide forms you have been given. You will be required to offer at least three objections. A time objection might be appropriate at the end of the presentation. Do not offer objections as questions but as statements. Ask appropriate questions, take an active part in the presentation, and make sure you sound conversational. Your instructor will inform you if you have to dress in any particular attire and if you can have the Planning Guide forms with you to refer to during the role play.

Guidelines for Being an Observer

If you are assigned the task of evaluating a presentation, use the Final Sales Presentation Rating Form on pages 125 and 126. If you will be evaluating a number of presentations, your instructor will give you several copies of the rating form. Fill out each section, as it is completed, rather than waiting until the end of the presentation. Space is provided between the skills for your comments. Evaluate the prospect as well as the salesperson.

Materials Needed to Role Play the Complete Presentation

Review the sections on the materials needed for the Approach (page 63), Securing Desire (page 75), Handling Objections (page 97), and Closing the Sale (page 116). These materials will be needed during the role play of the complete presentation.

Sales Presentation Written Report

Your instructor may require a written report of the sales presentation. The following discussion provides details of this assignment. Your completed Setting the Scene and Planning Guide forms from this text will contain most of the information needed for the report.

The sections in the report are listed below. These are the headings that should appear in the report. The format and nature of content in the Approach, Securing Desire, Handling Objections, and Closing the Sales sections should look exactly like the Planning Guide forms in the text for Fusion, including the headings and list of the steps.

(Title Page)

Executive Summary

Letter of Introduction

The Approach

Securing Desire

Handling Objections

Closing the Sale

Visual Aids

The title page should contain the following information centered on the page, all in bold font:

Sales Presentation For:

(name of company and product or service)

Submitted By:

(your name)

Submitted To:

(instructor's name)

(date the report is submitted)

(course name)

(day of the week and time the class meets)

The Executive Summary section of the report is a narrative (complete sentences and paragraphs) that provides an introduction to the report, nature of your sales presentation, and sources used to develop the presentation. Include a discussion of the following. Double-space the section.

❑ Purpose of the report

❑ Brief explanation of the sales presentation project

❑ Information from the Setting the Scene page in the text, written as a narrative

❑ Major sections in the report (see above) and a brief explanation of what is contained in each section

❑ Bibliography of sources used for information in the presentation. Ask your instructor what style of documentation should be used (e.g., MLA or APA.)

The Letter of Introduction is any communication that is sent to the prospect prior to the sales call. It prepares the prospect for a telephone or face-to-face call by the salesperson. The purpose of the letter is to arouse the prospect's interest and anticipation of the call. Refer to pages 21 and 22, where the Letter of Introduction is discussed. An example of a letter is also presented. Note the letter format.

The Approach section captures all the information in your completed Planning Guide form for the Approach, including the notation of the steps. Use the format below:

The Approach

Step 1. Introduction

SALESPERSON: (*Provide dialogue*)

PROSPECT: (*Provide dialogue*)

Step 2. Establish a rapport

SALESPERSON: (*Provide dialogue*)

PROSPECT: (*Provide dialogue*)

Step 3. . . . . .

The dialogue in each step should include each speaker, so have "SALESPERSON:" then dialogue and "PROSPECT:" then dialogue, like the Fusion example of the Approach.

The Securing Desire, Handling Objections, and Closing the Sale sections capture all of the information in your completed Planning Guides. Use the same format as described for the Approach above. Note where in the salesperson-prospect dialogue visual aids are shown to the prospect, for example, "(Show visual aid of a list of current customers.)" These notations should be in parentheses. The Planning Guides for each section of the Fusion presentation can serve as a guide.

All visual aids that are used in the presentation are to be contained in the Visual Aids section of the report. Visuals that you create must be typed, ensuring the text fills the entire page. Use bullet points where appropriate. Include a paragraph after the "Visual Aid" section heading that introduces the visual aids, explaining each in one sentence and identifying the section of the presentation where it is used. It is best to double-space this narrative section. The actual visual aids are to be attachments at the end of the report. Refer to pages 33 through 35 for a discussion of the visual aids that can be used.

The format of your report is extremely important. In addition to the format issues explained above, follow the guidelines below:

❑ Type the report, including any visual aids you created.

❑ Begin each section (e.g., Executive Summary, Letter of Introduction, Approach, Securing Desire, etc.) on a new sheet of paper.

❑ Use 12-point font for the report. Visual aids, however, usually require a much larger font.

❑ Section headings should stand out from the rest of the report. Print the report double-space except for the Letter of Introduction. Spacing may vary in the visual aids.

Assignments

1. The Web site for *Presentations* magazine is http://www.presentations.com. Visit the site and review articles on how to develop effective presentations. Develop a report on the site and what you learned from one article that is relevant to the sales presentation project. If you do not find a suitable article, go to a college or public library and search databases with full-text articles on features of an effective presentation. ABI/Inform is an example. The librarian may have to give you a password to access the databases.

2. Review the section in this chapter titled "Preparing to Role Play the Complete Presentation." Follow the directions and practice for the role play.

3. Prepare a typed report of your presentation. Refer to the section "Sales Presentation Written Report" in this chapter for guidelines.

Final Sales Presentation Rating Form (100 Points)

Salesperson's Company:_____   Hour:_____

Product/Service:_____   Salesperson's Name:_____

Prospect's Company:_____

Approach Skills	**Possible Score**	**Actual Score**
–Ability in wearing appropriate dress	5	_____
–Ability in introducing yourself and company, shaking the prospect's hand, offering a business card, and being seated	5	_____
–Ability in establishing a rapport, stating your purpose, and offering a general benefit	5	_____
–Ability in explaining your reason for needing information and offering fact-finding questions to determine the prospect's current situation	5	_____

Securing Desire Skills		
–Ability in briefly familiarizing the prospect with your company	5	_____
–Ability in asking questions to identify problems/needs and to confirm the prospect's desire to solve each one	5	_____
–Ability in providing features and benefits relevant to each problem/need and offering proof where appropriate	10	_____
–Ability in using visual or audio aids where appropriate and offering a trial close after each benefit statement	5	_____

Handling Objections Skills		
–Ability in acknowledging the prospect's concern and clarifying each objection	5	_____
–Ability in providing features and benefits relevant to each objection and offering proof where appropriate	10	_____
–Ability in using visual or audio aids where appropriate and offering a trial close after each objection	5	_____

Closing Skills

–Ability in recognizing buying signals and knowing when to ask a closing   5   _____
   question at each appropriate opportunity

–Ability in waiting for a response, recommending an order or plan of action,   5   _____
   and confirming the details

–Ability in reassuring the prospect, stating a follow-up plan, thanking the   5   _____
   prospect, and exiting properly

Other Skills

–Ability in maintaining the prospect's interest and attention throughout the   5   _____
   presentation and in getting the prospect involved

–Ability in using the prospect's name, power words, and picture words   5   _____

–Ability in projecting enthusiasm, poise, and confidence   5   _____

–Ability in maintaining good eye contact, smiling, and avoiding objectionable   5   _____
   mannerisms

                                                   Total   100 pts   _____

Prospect's Skills

Prospect's Name: _____

Ability in asking relevant questions, offering appropriate responses, and   10   _____
making the presentation sound conversational

Ability in being sufficiently demanding of the salesperson by offering at   10   _____
least three objections (A request for more information is not
considered an objection. No objections–0 points, 1 objection–3 points, 2
objections–6 points, and 3 or more objections–10 points.)

                                                   Total   20 pts.   _____